WORKING TOGETHER

A How-To-Do-It Manual for Trustees and Librarians

JAMES SWAN

HOW-TO-DO-IT MANUALS
FOR LIBRARIES
Number 24

NEAL-SCHUMAN PUBLISHERS, INC.
New York, London

Published by Neal-Schuman Publishers, Inc.
100 Varick Street
New York, NY 10013

Copyright © 1992 by James Swan

Printed and bound in the United States of America

Library of Congress Cataloging-in-Publication Data

Swan, James.
    Working together : a how-to-do-it manual for trustees and
librarians / James Swan.
        p. cm. — (How-to-do-it manuals for libraries ; no. 24)
    Includes bibliographical references and index.
    ISBN 1-55570-096-9 *55.00*
    1. Libraries—Trustees—Handbooks, manuals, etc.   2. Library
administration—Handbooks, manuals, etc.   I. Title.   II. Series.
Z681.5.S92   1992
021.8′2—dc20   92-19829
                                                                            CIP

This book is dedicated to the trustees and librarians of the Central Kansas Library System. Without their example and help, *Working Together* might never have happened.

CONTENTS

PREFACE

Why do we need another library trustee manual? Almost every state publishes one. They all tell trustees what to do, but very few tell them how to do it. The title of this book gives us the reason and the focus. *Working Together: A How-To-Do-It Manual for Librarians and Trustees* focuses on the relationship between the trustees and the librarian. When they work together, good things happen for their library. It is the only way to make them happen. The how-to-do-it aspect of the book is the extra step so many other manuals lack.

No book can overcome the obstreperousness of a controlling librarian or the laziness of a trustee who thinks that his or her only job is to come to the board meetings once a month and read the librarian's report. But if that is how librarians or trustees seem to you, this book can help.

Working is the first word in the title of this book because that's what it will take to make superb things happen for your library. I could have said *functioning,* or *operating,* or *meeting,* or *talking* instead of *working,* but those words don't convey the same energy. So as you read this book, look for ideas that will help your board and librarian work for solutions to the problems your library faces as it seeks to meet the needs of your community.

This book is about thresholds. Thresholds are windows of opportunity. Whether you create them or just take advantage of those that occur naturally is up to you. A threshold can be a chance meeting in the supermarket or on the golf course. It might be a telephone call from the librarian or another board member. It might even be the opportunity to say thank you to a benefactor. Your job is to look for thresholds of opportunity, and by doing so to make your library something better than it is today.

When I moved to Kansas several years ago, one of my board members tried to stump me with a bit of Kansas farm trivia. He asked me if I knew what a three-horse evener is. I didn't, so he told me that it was a device used to evenly distribute the workload of three horses hitched to a farm implement. It uses principles of physics to make sure that one horse doesn't have to match the effort of two horses hitched to the other side of whatever they are pulling. Working together is a little like a three-horse evener. Not everyone is capable of pulling the same weight, but when everyone pulls a share of the load, great things can happen in our libraries.

"The significant problems we face cannot be solved at the same level of thinking we were at when we created them," said Albert Einstein. (Covey 1989, 42) Look for some new ways to approach old problems. As you find new solutions, you will discover that changes in *your* attitude will make a difference in the outcome.

You need to find the answers for yourself. As you do, others will respond to the changes in your behavior. Who knows? They may choose to follow your new-found leadership skills. If they work, more power to you. If they don't, don't give up. Try something else.

INTRODUCTION

All glory comes from daring to begin.

Eugene F. Ware

You are a winner because you care about people and want them to work together. You care about your library and want it to be better than it is. This is the beginning of a great adventure for you. Would you like to:

- Have a new library?
- Set and accomplish exciting goals?
- Have more people use the library?
- See new ideas work?
- Have more money for your library?
- Enjoy greater public awareness?
- Feel greater public support for your library?

Whatever you want can be yours if you will set a goal and work for it—work for it together.

Maurice P. Marchant, Professor of Library and Information Science at Brigham Young University, said, "No *one* person can control what happens in a library. The librarian is not in control. The president of the board is not in control. The mayor is not in control. The efforts of the entire community control the destiny of the library." One person may prevent you from reaching your immediate goals, but eventually, if the community really wants a new library or an automated circulation system, working together will make it happen.

I have seen miracles happen because the board and the librarian became so focused on their goal that nothing could hold them back. In McCracken, Kansas (population 292), the roof on the old library leaked for ten years before they could raise $60,000 to build a new library. Fundraising was the key to their survival. They sold everything from note cards to cookbooks and solicited everyone in town and even those who had moved away. They succeeded because the librarian and the board of trustees *worked* together to make it happen.

In Glasco, Kansas (population 620), the library was crammed into 200 square feet of a modern city building. For years the board and librarian kept gentle pressure on the governing body to expand the library. Finally, after more than 12 years of friendly persuasion, the city council took advantage of an opportunity and made the library's dream come true. They bought a more spacious garage

THINGS TO DO

Likely or (not-so-likely) things to do at the library besides check out a book, video, or audiocassette:

Meet a friend
Escape from possible violence
Get a drink of water
Make a photocopy
Check the stock market
Take refuge from bad weather
Get help with homework
Read a magazine
Research a family tree
Look for job openings
Check on pending legislation
Attend a program on AIDS
Enjoy a movie with the family
Get a telephone number
Check the spelling of a word
Wait for parents after school
Get help filling out a tax form.
View a showing of local art
Type a resume

for their fire truck and moved it from the city building. They remodeled the space where the fire truck had been parked into a room for city council meetings and gave the old council room to the library. Everybody won, but it took years of working together. In this case the emphasis was on "together." Had the board played "hardball" with the governing body, they would probably still be in their cramped library.

PURPOSE OF WORKING TOGETHER

The title of this book, *Working Together*, begets the question, "For what purpose, or to what end, are we striving?" Every time the board or members of the board come together with the librarian to solve a library problem, they work together to give the people what they want when they go to the library. This observation silently asks the question we should ask ourselves every time a library patron walks through the front door: "What does this person need *this time*?" It could be something different every time.

Besides the lofty goals of lifelong learning, self-actualization, and self-esteem, we see more mundane, but no less important, purposes. Some people will want ideas for pet names, or how to grow tomatoes. On the more serious side, someone may be ill and want more information than their doctor has given them. I believe that every library should go beyond meeting the needs each patron brings to the library and create a new vision that reaches far into the community, offering choices and options. The message should be, "The library can help you do whatever you do better." That is the difference between being *reactive* and *proactive*. The reactive person says, "What do you need? Let me help you get it." The proactive person says, "I think people will need this" and then takes it to them.

As you read this book, think of the people who come to your library. Think of the people who don't come to your library. Think of their needs and how the library can help them. Every time you see the concept of working together mentioned in this book, ask yourself "What is the purpose of working together on this issue?"

FOR TRUSTEES

The purpose of this book is to help librarians and trustees rise to a new level of cooperation. When they understand the goals of the library they both serve, they will work together for their library. If you are a trustee, try reading *Working Together* from the viewpoint of the librarian. It could give you a new perspective. Several years ago I found a list of what employees look for in a job. Here it is ranked in order of importance:

1. Appreciation of their work
2. Being in on things
3. Having a boss who is sympathetic to personal problems
4. Job security
5. Good wages
6. Interesting work
7. Promotion and growth within the company
8. Management that is loyal to workers
9. Good working conditions
10. Tactful disciplining.

Trustees may find it difficult to try all of these ideas because they are not in daily contact with the library director, but the task of meeting the needs implied by this list will bring powerful results.

FOR LIBRARIANS, TOO

When I attend trustee programs at ALA conferences, I see as many library directors there as I see trustees. That is why this book is for librarians, too. If you are a librarian, look for ways to empathize with your board members and meet their needs. Consider their reasons for serving on the library board. They may:

- Want to be of service to the community
- Have a need to be needed
- Want to have some influence in library decisions
- Enjoy the library and want to give something back
- Feel an obligation to a friend who asked them to volunteer for the board.

If you don't know what their reasons for serving are, ask them. They will tell you, and the answer will help you work with them. Remember that most people do things because they want to, not because they have to.

Most trustees understand their role as the link between the library and the community. They are concerned about:

- Taxes
- Adequacy of funding for library service
- How well the library is meeting the needs of the people
- How well the library is communicating its services to the public

- How well the library is being managed
- How well the staff is treated.

Trustees have tremendous responsibilities. As you read this book, look for ways to help your board members. You may find passages you just can't wait to show your trustees. Restrain your enthusiasm. Just give them the book and let them find the passages on their own.

THE IMPORTANCE OF LEARNING
Trustees need an "everyday" perspective of library operations. They will be able to work with the librarian more effectively when they understand how a librarian thinks, and vice versa.

Think of this book as a workshop. As you read, imagine that your board has sent you away to a two-day workshop for library trustees. This workshop is filled with handouts, checklists, forms, and successful ideas that have worked for other library boards. As impressions come to you, jot them down, just as you would in a workshop. When you finish, you will return to your library with many action ideas you will want to try right away. You don't even have to finish the book to try out an idea. You could do something today that opens a door to something better.

THE ORIGIN OF *WORKING TOGETHER.*
In 1977 I moved to Kansas to become the director of the Great Bend Public Library and the Central Kansas Library System. The public library is operated by a seven-member administrative board, which is appointed by the mayor and ratified by the city council. The Central Kansas Library System is a 17- county cooperative with 60 autonomous public libraries. A major ongoing responsibility for me has been the training of 350 trustees. Every year I knew I would have from 75 to 100 newly appointed trustees to tutor in the ways of library work. Since 1977 I have conducted over 200 workshops on all phases of public library management. I have written and rewritten trustee manuals, handbooks, and workbooks. My article, "Inside the System: A Primer for Trustees" (*Wilson Library Bulletin,* February 1986), has been reprinted and distributed widely at state and national trustee meetings.

I have attended board meetings and consulted with librarians and trustees almost on a daily basis. The most important thing I learned from it all was that wherever the librarian and all the board members moved forward together with one purpose, success

BARRIERS TO WORKING TOGETHER

Adversarial stance
Complaining
Differing goals
Executive sessions
Failure to delegate responsibility
Fear of criticism
Hidden agendas
Lack of community awareness
Lack of enthusiasm
Lack of group skills
Lack of vision
Mistrust
Misunderstanding of roles
Non-attendance at meetings
One-person control
Personality conflicts
Poor leadership
Poorly defined goals
Power struggles
Prejudice
Resistance to change
Self-interest
Uncooperative attitudes
Uninterested board members
Weak communication

followed. Wherever there was a division between board members or wherever there were feelings of antagonism between the librarian and the board, everything stagnated. The library failed to progress. Public support waned. Circulation declined. The library suffered from benign neglect.

This book is designed to be the "first read" for the newly appointed trustee or the librarian who trains newly appointed board members. I hope my ideas on library trusteeship make you feel enthusiastic about the opportunity you have to work with other trustees and your librarian. I hope the charts, forms, checklists, and sample documents will make it easier to apply the ideas you find in the book. Though *Working Together* is not an exhaustive study of the topic, you will find enough detailed suggestions to keep yourself busy for years. If you need more information than you find in this book, check the bibliography. It lists resources that have been helpful to me in my work with trustees.

EVERY VACANCY IS AN OPPORTUNITY FOR GROWTH

For things to improve, it was often necessary to get a new librarian. Sometimes everyone had to wait for a powerful, controlling trustee to rotate off the board. I have seen some dramatic shifts in library service and public response as a result of personnel changes.

In my workshops, I also learned that it is better not to exclude librarians from the programs for trustees. For years our trustee workshops were "trustees-only" events. Librarians automatically wondered what kind of "skullduggery" was being cooked up against them. Recently I began inviting librarians to attend the trustee workshops and have involved them in designing ways to create a cooperative environment with their boards. Involving librarians in the workshops broke down barriers of distrust, even though it occasionally made it difficult to deal with trustee concerns about, for example, a librarian who is rude to clients. Perhaps the way to handle such a concern expressed by an individual trustee is to have a one-on-one session with the trustee or perhaps the librarian. The answers are here in this book. Read on!

WORKSHOP RESPONSES

In a series of trustee workshops, I asked the participants to share with me what they saw as barriers to working together. Their list was very enlightening.

Might your library have one or more of these barriers? Would

BENEFITS OF WORKING TOGETHER

Better library service
Board members take active part
Can set common goals
Cooperation happens
Easier to fill seats on board
Fundraising easier
Good attitude
Greater community awareness
Greater staff morale
Growth
Improved communications
Improved public relations/image
It's more fun to work together
Librarian takes action
Librarian's job more pleasant
Meeting needs of community
Money comes to library
More people come to library
More visibility for library programs
New ideas become workable
New library generates new
    business/gifts/people
No one person does everything
People are willing to invest more
    time and energy
Pleasant conditions
Positive public image
Satisfying patrons
Seeking new opinions
Sharing of ideas
Trustees know what's going on
Trustees stay interested
We are well informed
We have a team
We usually get job done

you like to know how to fix it? This book contains positive helps for trustees and librarians who want to establish a more cooperative relationship with their librarian and other board members.

In the same workshop, I asked the participants to tell me how their library benefited from working together. That list was just as helpful.

SOME INSPIRING CASE HISTORIES

As part of the research for this book, I sent out a short survey to people who had been identified as having accomplished something outstanding because they had worked together. (I have quoted their responses with permission.) Most of the libraries succeeded at building a new library, adding to an existing one, or installing an automated circulation system. Despite what could have been overwhelming odds, participants accomplished their goals.

A Success Story in Pennsylvania: In 1974 the western Pocono area of Pennsylvania was totally without library service. Today it has a beautiful library with a budget of over $150,000. More than 25 volunteers keep the library open 35 hours a week.

Carol H. Kern, Director of the Western Pocono Community Library in Brodheadsville, reports that in 1974 the nearest library was as far as 40 minutes travel time for some residents. A group of volunteers decided to incorporate and organize a library that could serve their needs more effectively. Strictly through volunteer effort a library grew—with an annual budget in 1974 of about $2,000 and a budget today of $150,000. The library occupies a building of about 3,000 square feet on one acre of land and serves almost 10,000 patrons. This is remarkable in view of the fact that in 1974 there were fewer than 5,000 people in the entire service area. Today that area has almost 18,000 people.

The key to success of the library was the commitment of competent volunteers and the fact that no bureaucratic actions blocked the way of progress. The staff remained totally volunteer for almost 15 years. Resources were thus directed toward the purchase of books and other library materials. During those formative years, the volunteers felt it was more important for the library to buy books than to pay staff. The regional library center in Easton, Pennsylvania, was extremely supportive in providing professional guidance and resources and never attempted to do anything but encourage the library in its efforts. While other libraries were cutting services due to declining funding, the Western Pocono library's volunteers gave generously of their time.

Their advice to others who may want to try the same thing is, "Don't let bureaucrats or other libraries intimidate you and undercut your efforts because your community library lacks professional credentials. The key to success is service, and many professionals have forgotten this. Librarians must learn how to smile when they deal with the general public."

Automation Project in Colorado: Peg Carlson, trustee from the Fort Lupton Public and School Library in Fort Lupton, Colorado, tells how people connected with the library worked together to install an automated circulation system. "In 1988 it became obvious that the automated circulation system then in use was inadequate for our needs. Wild Library District was installing a Dynix System, which would accommodate member libraries, including our library. After considering possible solutions, the director presented three suggestions to the board of trustees: 1) go back to manual circulation procedures; 2) purchase a system that would tie into the school district, since our library is in the high school building; or 3) somehow find the money to join the Wild Library District's Dynix System. The board decided to join the Dynix System, which would give our local patrons access to hundreds of thousands of books. Money would have to be found from sources other than the school district and the city, which support the library on an 80/20 percent split. The library board told the director to apply for an LSCA (Library Services and Construction Act) grant and approved interest returns from a trust account managed by the library for use in supporting the grant. Both the library trustees and the library director collaborated in preparing the grant proposal. The trustees also approved use of a memorial gift for the project. The library received the LSCA grant and a special grant from the Wild Library District, enabling us to go on line with the new system in the fall of 1990.

"The keys to the success of the project: an excellent LSCA grant proposal was written by the library director with the help of trustees; the Wild Library District director and board of trustees gave support and financial help; and the High Plains Regional Library Service System aided the library staff and trustees in weeding the collection before installation of the new system."

Peg Carlson's advice to others is to "seek more money to provide on-site training by the computer company personnel for employees directly involved in circulation. Those employees are the ones who serve the customers and generate good will and PR on behalf of the library. It is imperative that they understand the shortcuts and the system."

Greater Support in Vermont: You may not need to build a $2 million library. Perhaps all you need is a little more money for books and operations. The principle of working together can have a valuable impact in smaller projects, too.

Pat Hazelhurst, librarian of the Colbleigh Public Library, Lyndonville, Vermont, shares her experience: "Town support for the library was minimal. Working together, the librarian and trustees launched an effort to gain the needed support. They conducted a survey, documented statistics of use, and generated and adopted a plan for service."

Their key to success was community involvement. Everyone worked to increase awareness for the role of the library, which resulted in increased funding approved by the town.

They started with statistical documentation to prove the need and followed it with continuous communication between the board, the librarian, and the town governing body.

Pat Hazelhurst continues, "The town selectmen were informed of our progress periodically, and the public was encouraged to communicate their approval of the library to the governing body. The town government decided that the library was an important part of town life, included the library in its regular budget (as opposed to being an add-on item), and increased monetary support by 100 percent over a two-year period."

Their only word of advice to others seeking to increase their budgets the same way: "Have patience!"

Everyone Wins in Texas: Kathleen Metson, Librarian of the Rockwall County Library in Texas, tells how the library board was able to go beyond the trustee/librarian relationship to involve the governing bodies of both the city and the county to produce a real win/win situation that resulted in a spacious new library:

"For the past 11 years the Rockwall County Library has been housed in a 2800-square-foot building with no way to expand. Although Rockwall County is the smallest county in the state, it is the fastest growing. The library was in desperate need of a larger building. The last local bond issues (city, county, and school district) had all failed.

"The old post office in the City of Rockwall became available from the federal government. The city and the county were bidding against each other for the building. The Rockwall County Library Board and the librarian unanimously decided to approach both the county and the city with the idea of jointly purchasing the building and using part of it for a new library.

"The library board president presented our proposal to the

County Commissioners and the City Council. Both bodies eventually agreed to have representatives meet and try to negotiate an agreement. The resulting joint bid was accepted by the federal government in January 1990.

"The library board and the librarian agreed that we had to compromise. The post office building was actually smaller than we needed. However, we knew it would be futile to try another bond issue in the present economy. So we decided to go ahead with the post office, which would at least triple our space and allow us to expand the collection and services.

"The real key to our successful campaign is twofold: 1) our board president knows many of the commissioners and council members and is very persuasive; 2) the timing was right. There were people on both the court (county governing body) and the council (city governing body) who saw the need for a new library. The ability of the two bodies to cooperate was very important to the success of the project.

"Everything went well. We haven't had a real snag since the beginning. Even our architect says he has never worked on a project where everyone was in agreement as they are here. Once after the property had been acquired and the architect chosen, there was a small faction objecting to the cost of remodeling. The librarian, the board, and the Friends started a telephone campaign and had people speak at a public meeting of Commissioners Court. The support was overwhelming. In fact, no one from the opposition even spoke."

Ms. Metson's advice to those who may try this type of project is: "Be willing to compromise. Make sure the timing is right. Don't underestimate the value of good public relations."

Working Together in Connecticut: One of my survey letters serendipitously led me to a pamphlet called "Working Together" recently published jointly by the Connecticut State Library, Association of Connecticut Library Boards, and Friends of Connecticut Libraries. They have graciously given their permission to use the publication in my version of *Working Together* (see Figure 1).

QUESTIONNAIRE RESULTS
In one of the questionnaires I sent to trustees and librarians in the Central Kansas Library System, I asked, "How would you suggest that the librarian and library board work together to make your library more responsive to the needs of the community?" Here are some of their responses:

FIGURE 1 Connecticut's "Working Together" Brochure, Outside

Working Together

CONNECTICUT STATE
CSL
LIBRARY

**AC
LB**

**Friends of
Connecticut
Libraries**

April 1991

Funded through the Library Services and Construction Act

Notes:

Connecticut State Library
231 Capitol Ave.
Hartford, CT 06106

Non-Profit Org.
U.S. Postage
PAID
Permit No.

Hartford, CT

FIGURE 1 *Cont'd.* Connecticut's Brochure, Inside

Responsibilities of	Library Director	Trustee	Friend
General Administrative	Administer daily operation of the library including personnel, collection development, fiscal, physical plant and programmatic functions. Act as technical advisor to the board and ensure staff representation at all friends' board meetings.	Recruit and employ a qualified library director; maintain an ongoing performance appraisal process for the director.	Support quality library service in the community through fund raising, volunteerism and serving as advocates for the library's program.
Policy	Apprise board of need for new policies, as well as policy revisions; implement the policies of the library as adopted by the board; keep friends apprised of all library policies.	Identify and adopt written policies to govern the operation and program of the library including personnel, general operating, and collection development policies.	Support the policies of the library as adopted by the library board; adopt a constitution and by-laws for the friends.
Planning	Coordinate and implement long range planning process with board, friends, staff and community. Long range plan coordination will include preparation of appropriate status reports.	Ensure that the library has a long range planning process with implementation and evaluation components. The process should include input from friends, community and staff. Support the librarian, staff and friends in carrying out the library's program.	Provide input into library's long range planning process and remain knowledgeable as to the status of the plan.
Marketing	Coordinate and implement an ongoing marketing program.	Ensure that the library has an active marketing program.	Promote the library program to the public.
Fiscal	Prepare an annual budget for the library in consultation with the board and friends; present current report of expenditures against the budget at each board meeting; make the friends aware of the special financial needs of the library.	Secure adequate funds to carry out the library's program; assist in the preparation and presentation of the annual budget.	Conduct fund raising which complements the library's mission and provides funding for special library projects.
Legislative	Educate board and friends regarding current local, state and federal library laws and pending library legislation.	Be familiar with local, state and federal library laws as well as pending library legislation.	Serve as advocates for local, state and national library issues; represent the library program to legislators.
Meetings	Provide written reports at and participate in all board and friends meetings; ensure that there is a staff liaison to the friends.	Attend and participate in all board meetings and see that accurate records are kept on file at the library; comply with Freedom of Information regulations; appoint a liaison to the friends' board to attend their meetings.	Maintain a liaison to the board of trustees to attend all their meetings. Executive board members should attend and participate in all friends' executive board meetings.
Networking	Affiliate with the state and national professional organizations and attend professional meetings and workshops; make use of the services and consultants of the Connecticut State Library, Association of Connecticut Library Boards, Inc. and Friends of Connecticut Libraries, Inc.	Attend regional, state, and national trustee meetings and workshops, and affiliate with the appropriate professional organizations. Make use of the services of the Connecticut State Library and Association of Connecticut Library Boards, Inc.	Affiliate with state and national friends' organizations and attend their meetings and workshops. Make use of the services and consultants of the Connecticut State Library as well as Friends of Connecticut Libraries, Inc.

- Keep communication lines open.
- Show appreciation for work well done.
- Listen for public comments.
- Encourage a good relationship with the press.
- Work to make the public more aware of the library's value.
- Try to fit library services and programs to the needs of all age groups.
- Be quick to explain actual needs of the library to the public.
- Schedule regular events at the library.
- Get as many people as possible to come to the library for something! Anything!
- Put a suggestion box in library.
- Try to give the people what they want when they come to the library.
- The board should learn the feelings and concerns of the public and express them to the library.
- Go to the community organizations and find out how the library can be of use.
- Begin a volunteer program so people can work for the library and feel more responsible for it.
- Hold an open house and invite the public to meet board members.
- Do not let personal thoughts interfere with group decisions.
- Board members should be aware of the professional responsibilities of librarians.

PRINCIPLES FOR WORKING TOGETHER

Many of these ideas have found their way into the fabric of *Working Together*. The following are my principles for working together:

1. Start with a goal that can be perceived as a benefit to the public. Working together without a purpose is spinning your wheels.
2. Start by enlisting 100 percent support from everyone on the board.
3. Expand the planning group to include community leaders and library staff.
4. Be prepared to include new ideas as part of the major goal.
5. Communicate honestly and openly. Tell everyone (including the governing body) everything at every step of the process. Make sure the groups are talking to each other.
6. Be honest and consistent. Don't tell one group one thing and another group something else.

7. Be patient. Allow time for new ideas to sink in and change the thinking of those whose ideas need to change.
8. Look for win/win opportunities.
9. Be willing to work! If everyone is not committed to the project enough to work for it, be prepared to fail.

THUMB RULES

Donald B. Reynolds, Assistant Administrator of the Central Kansas Library System, developed a set of "thumb rules" for working with people. They address some essential needs in positive human relationships.

The Count de Buffon, an eighteenth century naturalist, once said that the cat "appears to have feelings only for himself, loves only conditionally, and only enters into relations [with people] in order to abuse them." A wag has suggested that most supervisors behave similarly. Now, although that may be a bit overstated, there are times when people working together do get into abusive habits. In order to short-circuit that kind of behavior, there are some rules of thumb which might be helpful to remember in our relations with one another.

1. *Each of us has control of our own lives.* Who we are is who we want to be. What we do is what we truly mean. Being reactive instead of active keeps our minds in neutral rather than drive. We acquiesce by our silence to what others do if we don't speak up for our ideas and our feelings. Silence is indeed assent.
2. *To find answers and get information, ask questions.* If we ask not, we will never find out why. If we don't know why something is happening, it is better to ask than to sit around grumbling that "nobody ever tells me anything." By saying that, we indicate our lack of interest in searching for ourselves.
3. *Clear up gripes as soon as possible.* If we have a gripe or complaint about what is being done or the way things are going, we should share our feelings with the person in charge of that area to see if a change can be made. If not, we should examine what in us is causing our irritation and possibly change our attitude. A continuing gripe signals our unwillingness to take a positive self-action.
4. *Monday morning quarterbacking is unhealthy for the soul.* It's very easy to point out the errors of other's ways and what could or should have been done after it's all over and the decision(s) made. If we don't care for the result, we

should keep it to ourselves unless continuing evaluation and development are called for and allow for future change.

5. *Reliving the past is toxic.* The past is over, and we can't do anything more about it. So forget it.

6. *Say what you mean and really listen to others.* We must learn to transmit our thoughts clearly and to listen to our colleagues in order to grasp the real meaning of what they're telling us. We must listen to nuances and be aware of hidden meanings in our own messages. We have words to express and explain our feelings; vague allusions or joking phrases are inappropriate. Words are hard to find sometimes, yet they are our best vehicles for communicating ideas and sharing feelings. It is unfair of us to expect others to be able to read our minds or our body language when we won't say what we mean. The very act of talking can often clarify our meanings. What we say may be repeated and we may be quoted. Is what we say what we want others to hear?

7. *There is no mysterious "they."* We are all in this together. We are they.

8. *Don't be disturbed.* Nobody or nothing can upset us or cause us stress. It is only what we feel about people and events that can bring disturbance. If we look for and expect the best, we will find it—almost all the time. We are what we think.

9. *Be of good cheer.* A giggle a day keeps the "gloomies" away. A glad heart makes a cheerful countenance; a cheerful heart is a good medicine. We are as happy or unhappy, content or miserable as we suppose ourselves to be.

SUMMARY

Stephen Covey in his audiocassette seminar, *Seven Basic Habits of Highly Effective People,* suggests new ways of looking at the world—a paradigm shift. I hope *Working Together* will give you a new vision for the word *cooperation.* As you find ideas you would like to try, take a minute and jot them down on the Action Plan on the next page. Whether you want to build a new library or revise your library policy, try Dr. Covey's *Seven Basic Habits.* Here they are:

- *Be proactive.* Do something. Act rather than being acted upon.

- *Begin with the end in mind.* Set goals. Work to achieve them.
- *Put first things first.* It is more important to do the right things than to do things right.
- *Think win/win.* Work for ways to help others win while accomplishing your own goals.
- *Seek first to understand (then to be understood).* Learn to listen and understand the other point of view.
- *Synergize.* Work to make the whole more than the sum of its parts. This is the essence of working together.
- *Sharpen the saw.* Take time to develop the physical, emotional/social, spiritual, and mental aspects of your life.

These seven habits are at the root of every cooperative effort. To be truly effective as a library board/librarian combination you have to *work* at these habits and you have to do it *together*. Get a copy of Dr. Covey's book or the cassette seminar. It could be the best thing you ever did for your library.

Action Plan

Working Together Idea	How can I change the idea to make it work in my library?	When will I do it?

REVIEWING TRUSTEE AND LIBRARIAN ROLES

Anything that can be misunderstood has been misunderstood.

Murphy

Trustees need accurate information to help them make decisions that will benefit their library. Your job is to get the information you need and participate in the decision-making process. If you do it well and work with the other members of your team, your library will grow, improve, and become a source of community pride. If not, it will suffer. Remember that your primary purpose as a trustee is to work for the betterment of your library and its services to the public.

GETTING STARTED

The first person you want to talk with upon becoming a trustee is your librarian. He or she is your link to the staff and the library. Better than anyone else, librarians know what is going on in the library. Ask for a tour of the library. It will reveal much about your library *and* about the librarian. The librarian who doesn't want to show you the mess in the storage room may not want you to see the bookkeeping mess in the office either. Your librarian should be honest with you about the strengths of the library as well as its limitations.

Brush up on your listening skills. Learn to say "I see" and "Tell me more." Then summarize what you are hearing to make sure you understand. Ask about library programs and make positive comments about what you see. Ask, "What is going well for the library?" Find out what areas need help.

After you have seen the children's room, the charging system, and the card catalog, ask to see the furnace room and the magazine storage area. Trustees are responsible for the *whole* library. The roof and carpeting are big-ticket items that can deplete a library's budget if plans are not in place to allow for their replacement.

After the tour, ask your librarian for your copy of the board manual. If your library doesn't have one, now might be a good time to develop one. You may not have the skill, right now, to tackle the task yourself, but if you set a goal and work with the librarian, you could produce a very helpful document in a year or so.

After you talk with the librarian and read the board manual, call the president of the board and ask specific questions. You won't become an expert overnight, but your interest in and knowledge about the library will impress others at the first board meeting. Your interest sends a signal to them that you are preparing to make a valuable contribution.

MAKING DECISIONS

As a trustee you are responsible for your library's well-being. You will carry out your task by making decisions in five basic areas:

1. Hiring and working with the librarian
2. Creating policy
3. Managing money
4. Carrying out public relations
5. Planning.

Library boards discuss and decide library matters in one or more of these categories at their monthly meetings. Your job is to attend every board meeting. You cannot contribute if you are not there.

Before the board meeting the librarian or board secretary should send you:

1. Last month's minutes
2. A financial statement
3. The librarian's report
4. This month's board meeting agenda
5. Any special documents pertinent to the meeting.

This one effort can save hours at the board meeting. Prepare for the meeting by reading the material. Ask for the material if you don't get it before the meeting.

HIRING THE LIBRARIAN

The opportunity to hire a new librarian may happen only once while you are on the board, so consider your decision carefully. The person you hire will set the tone for the library for the next several years. Try to hire someone who is pleasant to be around.

Qualifications are important. If your library can afford a person with a master's degree in library science, then hire one. If you can't afford someone with an M.L.S., look for a person with a college degree who loves books and reading. People skills are important, too. Find someone who is personable and outgoing. Remember, you are looking for someone who will work *with* the board, not *for* the board.

WORKING WITH YOUR LIBRARIAN

What do you do if you inherit a librarian with shortcomings? Instituting performance appraisal won't work. If you are unhappy with your librarian's present performance, starting a performance appraisal program will probably make things worse. It won't change the problem behavior.

Behavior modification through motivation might help, but you must remember that you cannot easily change other people's behavior. If you change your own behavior, others will respond to the changes in you. If your librarian never smiles or says "Good morning," find out how entrenched the behavior is. Does one board member in seven receive a smile and greeting? Set a goal that the librarian will smile and greet everyone warmly, including all board members. Data collection requires that board members visit the library often so they can collect the data—smiles or frowns, warm greetings or grumbles. The first board member to receive a smile and "Good morning" positively reinforces the behavior by saying, "It makes me feel good to come to the library and be greeted so warmly." And so on through the board. The librarian will soon get the idea. Feedback is passing on positive comments from others. Soon being on the "friendly team" will be the thing to do. This sounds simple, but it works. Transfer the technique to other targeted behaviors. The principles are constant.

Smooth operation of the library depends on the relationship between the board and the librarian. Start by clearly separating the responsibilities of the board and the role of the librarian. *The Library Trustee: A Practical Guidebook* by Virginia Young (Bowker, 1978) is an excellent resource for delineating the differences. Also, you may want to contact the American Library Trustee Association, 50 East Huron, Chicago Illinois 60611, for additional information about the duties of a library trustee. The board sets policy and hires a competent librarian. The librarian carries out the policy set by the board and runs the library. If everyone follows the rules, everything works fine—or at least it is supposed to!

Conflicts arise when board members take over the role of the librarian and start meddling in daily business or when the librarian usurps more authority than has been granted by the board. If staff members are allowed to communicate directly with board members about their concerns, the process can undermine the authority of the librarian. *Definition of Administrative Roles by Position,* Appendix E may help the board and the library director establish normal channels of communication on a variety of library interactions.

If trustees have to step in to conduct daily business because the librarian isn't doing the job, maybe you need a new librarian. But be careful! If you get to the point of firing your librarian, document every effort to correct the problem. Written reprimands and warnings should be signed by the recipient and the president of the board. It might pay to consult the library's lawyer before taking action against the librarian.

Establish a policy and procedure for dismissals, then follow it. Clearly define the grounds for dismissal and carefully word the warning procedure. You can be sued if you fire a librarian for capricious or unjustified reasons, but remember you do have a right to have a competent person working for the library.

If you decide to work with performance appraisal, make sure you do it with a competent, self-confident librarian who really cares about the library. For some librarians, performance appraisals only confirm feelings of low self-esteem.

A good performance appraisal document is based upon the job description. It lists the basic tasks of the position and describes what will happen when the task is done well. Your librarian will have an important role in determining the specifics. The board then reviews the standards with the librarian, making positive suggestions for changes. Remember that performance appraisal should be continuous and ongoing. "No surprises" should be the rule. It is not fair to withhold uncommunicated expectations and then spring them on the employee in the evaluation.

CREATING POLICY

Just about everything the library board does relates to policy. Policy often determines priorities for the budget. Policy affects librarians and their relationship with the staff members. Policies are the basis for programs. Think about it, and count the number of motions that relate to policies at your next board meeting. Policies should not be a rigid set of rules, but a blueprint or roadmap for library operations. Written policies let the public and staff know the library's position. They should be clearly written and understandable to all.

A positively worded book selection policy, based on "The Library Bill of Rights" and the "Freedom to Read Statement," is a

THE VALUE OF ESTABLISHED POLICY

A policy written after the fact can do little to correct a bad situation, while a well-written policy already in place can do much to keep a minor skirmish from developing into a major battle.

real friend in the face of a censorship challenge. If you are armed beforehand, the battle could be over before it starts.

Good staff morale is critical to a well-run library. When you review the personnel policy, allow for as much staff input as possible. Be especially careful when it comes to vacation, sick leave, health insurance, or some other perquisite that is already enjoyed by the staff.

Policy should be flexible and subject to change, with a regularly scheduled review to guarantee that it meets current situations. Ten years ago most libraries didn't need policies on computers, video-tape collections, or database searching, but today these services are part of most library programs.

MANAGING MONEY

Once the budget is set by the board, it is the librarian's job to manage the library's money. The board should receive and review a monthly financial statement. Board members should ask questions if they have any and then vote to approve the monthly bills and file the financial statements for the auditor.

The library board's primary money management role is to allocate current resources. The librarian and the board work together to develop the annual budget. The librarian is in the library every day and knows what books people read or when the roof leaks. The librarian usually makes purchases, verifies the expenditures to the board, and brings invaluable information to budget discussions. The board works with that information and sets the budget for the year.

Budgeting is the process of allocating available resources. First priority usually goes to those line items over which we have very little control. Second priority is for those items over which we have absolute control. Utilities, building maintenance, and salaries tend to claim a lion's share of the money, while the rest is spent on books, materials, and programs.

The board's role is to secure adequate funding. The board must constantly strike a balance between asking for more of available tax money and considering the needs of the library. If tax funds are inadequate or if you just need some ideas on how to get more money for your library, obtain a copy of my book, *Fundraising for the Small Public Library: A How-To-Do-It Manual for Librarians* (Neal-Schuman, 1990). Most of the information is applicable to any organization, including a public library of any size. It is filled with practical ideas to help any organization find more money— and is especially helpful if you are planning a capital fund drive for a building project.

EXAMINING STATE LIBRARY LAWS

- What is the process for becoming a library trustee?
- What role does the library board have in the process?
- What are the terms of office? (How long can you serve on the library board?)
- What happens if someone is not appointed to take your place after your term expires?
- What is the mayor's role (if any) on the library board?
- What is the role of other members of the governing body?
- What are the residency requirements for trustees?
- What, if any, is the compensation for library trustees?
- Under what circumstance may you be sued as a board member?
- What does the law say about time and place of meetings?
- Under what conditions may a special meeting be called?

The budget is the library's single most important planning document because it is the basis for the monthly financial statement. Knowing the library's current financial situation will help you determine future expenditures. If utility costs are running higher than normal, you know you will have to cut back somewhere else to balance the budget at the end of the year. The board helps the librarian make these decisions.

CARRYING OUT PUBLIC RELATIONS

Everything we do creates an image in someone's mind. Good or bad, like it or not, we all have public relations. Our job is to create a positive image of the library. Although the librarian is usually the chief public relations officer for the library, there is much trustees can do to further the cause of the library. Trustees see the library from the public's viewpoint. In fact every time they enter the library, they should try to see it as a newcomer sees it. Is the library comfortable and inviting? Are staff members friendly and helpful? Are you drawn to attractive displays that make you want to pick up books and read them? If the answer is yes, then tell others! If the answer is no, then tell the librarian. When people come to the library they should feel comfortable and welcome.

Trustees are influential people. Outside the library, they make those all-important face-to-face contacts. They can work with community leaders in ways the librarian cannot. Sometimes efforts by the librarian to increase funding are seen as self-serving, but trustees usually serve without pay, so their efforts are seen in a different light. Public relations is creating a positive image by working with people.

Learn all you can about the current political scene. Learn how it works and where the library fits in the order of local priorities. "Politics" is not a dirty word, but a way of getting things done through people. Learn to make the politics work *for* your library.

PLANNING

Planning is intellectual creation. When we plan, we create what we want to happen through vision and concentration. We need enough imaginative power to envision what the finished product will be. The library's goals and objectives provide us with purpose and direction for the future. Here is a concise outline for organizational planning:

- Write down the organization's mission statement
- Develop goals for your organization based on the mission statement

EXAMINING STATE LIBRARY LAWS, Cont'd.

- How does the open meetings law in your state apply to libraries?
- Must the treasurer be bonded?
- Who may sign checks for payment of obligations?
- How do the laws for your size library differ from libraries larger than yours? Smaller than yours?
- What is the basis of funding for your library?
- Who determines how much money the library will have to spend?
- How can the library get more tax money?
- How is state aid determined?
- What are the laws governing the investment of public funds?
- What reports are required by your municipality?
- What reports are required by the state library?
- What reports are required by your system headquarters?

- Create objectives for each goal
- Devise action plans for each objective
- Set a budget for each action plan
- Evaluate your success or failure
- Restate your goals and objectives
- Repeat the process

Successful planning is cyclical and ongoing. Once you complete an action plan, it is time to evaluate your success and start over.

Be aware of costs. Once we had a great publicity idea. We developed a place mat to give local cafes to advertise library services, but found that it cost too much to implement at that time. Budgeting for the project brought us face to face with our priorities. Your library budget is your most important planning document. Use it to help with planning.

Patrick Hagerty of Texas Instruments said, "Those who implement the plans must make the plans." Library boards need to involve their librarians in library planning. After all, the librarian is the chief implementer of the plans. Helping to make the plans, the librarian "buys into the deal" and has a personal stake in the outcome. The success of the library is what the trustee/librarian team is all about.

LEGAL QUESTIONS

It is no surprise that library laws are different in every state; they are even different for various public libraries within a state. It is beyond the scope of *Working Together* to cite library law as it exists in every state. Find out about library laws in your own state and make sure that your library board operates within those laws. Check with your state library. Almost every state has a public library trustee manual. You might believe that there is very little you can do about the law in your state. Not so! Every legislative session is a window of opportunity. By working together with other library leaders in your state, you have the opportunity to change the law. Although it may take a few years to see a change in the law, don't give up. You can make a difference.

Why do you need the answers to all of these questions? To help you to ask: "How can I use this information to work with other people and make things better for my library?" If you know how money is allocated to your library, you can use that information to increase funding for your library. Every state is different; even municipalities within states are different. Your librarian should know the answer to most of the questions. Additionally, most

RESPONSIBILITIES OF TRUSTEES

1. To employ a competent and qualified librarian

2. To determine the purpose of the library and to adopt written policies to govern the operation and program of the library

3. To establish, support, and participate in a planned public relations program

4. To assist in the preparation of the annual budget and approve the final document

5. To know local and state laws and to actively support library legislation on the state and national levels

6. To establish library policies for dealing with books and materials selection

7. To attend all board meetings and ascertain that accurate records are kept on file at the library

8. To attend regional, state, and national trustee meetings and workshops, and to affiliate with appropriate professional organizations

9. To establish policies that encourage use of system services

10. To be aware of the services of the state library

11. To report regularly to the governing officials and the general public

12. To determine the program and needs of the library in relation to the community and to keep abreast of standards and library trends

13. To secure adequate funds to carry on the library program

RESPONSIBILITIES OF LIBRARIANS

1. To act as technical advisor to the board and to recommend employment of all personnel and supervise their work

2. To carry out the policies of the library as adopted by the board and to recommend needed policies for board action

3. To maintain an active program of public relations

4. To prepare an annual budget for the library in consultation with the board and to give a current report of actual expenditures against the budget at each meeting

5. To know local and state laws and to actively support library legislation in the state and nation

6. To select and order all books and other library materials according to board policy

7. To attend all board meetings and to serve as secretary of the board if required

8. To affiliate with state and national professional organizations, attend professional meetings and workshops, and provide professional development opportunities for the staff

9. To make full use of system services

10. To utilize the services and consultants of the state library

11. To report regularly to the library board, to the officials of local government, and to the general public

12. To suggest and carry out plans for extending services of the library

13. To prepare regular reports detailing current progress and future needs of the library

---

FIGURE 1-1 Summary of Survey Results

As part of the research for this book, I conducted a mail survey of the library development consultants in every state library, to establish the background for working together in each state.

The following is a summary of the responses I received:

Library Trustee Law, Selection, and Authority

Boards of trustees

Do public libraries in the state have boards of trustees?

State Statute

Does state statute specify method of selection, terms of office and authority, etc. of public library trustees?

Method of selection

1. Elected.
2. Appointed by mayor and ratified by governing body.
3. Appointed by elected official without ratification of a governing body.
4. Nominated by the board of trustees and sustained by governing body.
5. Nominated by the board of trustees and elected by the same body.
6. Appointed directly by governing body.

Type of authority

Autonomous: Authority to levy taxes as needed, set the budget, control expenditures, set salaries, hire the librarian, and generally operate the library free of intervention from any other agency. Answers only to the public.

Administrative: Authority to set the budget within funding limitations established by statute, control expenditures, set salaries, hire the librarian, and generally operate the library free of intervention from other agencies or directors.

Policy Making: Authority to set policy for library operations. Make recommendations to another agency or governing body on the budget, hiring the librarian, personnel policies, and staffing.

Advisory: Make recommendations to governing body or someone in city government regarding library budget, library personnel, and policy. Main function is to represent the thinking of the public regarding public policy for the library.

	Boards of Trustees	State Statute	Method of Selection	Type of Authority
Alabama	Yes	Yes	6	Administrative
Alaska	Yes*	No	2	Administrative
Arizona	Yes	Yes	3	Advisory
Arkansas	Yes	Yes	2	Policy

FIGURE 1-1 *Cont'd.*

	Boards of Trustees	State Statute	Method of Selection	Type of Authority
California	Yes	Yes	1,2,3	Advisory
Colorado	Yes	Yes	2,4	Administrative, Advisory
Connecticut	Yes	Yes	1,2,4,5	Administrative, Policy, Advisory
Delaware	Yes	Yes	4,5	Advisory
Florida	Yes	No	3	Advisory
Georgia	Yes	Yes	6	Administrative
Hawaii	No	N/A	N/A	N/A
Idaho	Yes	Yes	1,3	Autonomous, Administrative
Illinois	Yes	Yes	1, 2	Autonomous, Administrative
Indiana	Yes	Yes	6	Administrative
Iowa	Yes	Suggested	2	Administrative
Kansas	Yes	Yes	2,3	Autonomous, Administrative
Kentucky	Yes	Yes	6	Autonomous
Louisiana	Yes	Yes	3	Administrative, Policy
Maine	Yes	No	5	Policy
Maryland	Yes	Yes	3,5	Policy
Massachusetts	Yes	Yes	1,2,3,4,5	Administrative
Michigan	Yes	Yes	2,3	Administrative
Minnesota	Yes	Yes	2*	Administrative
Mississippi	Yes	Yes	6	Administrative, Advisory
Missouri	Yes	Yes	2,3,5,6	Autonomous
Montana	Yes	Yes	3	Administrative
Nebraska	Yes	Yes	6	Administrative
Nevada	Yes	Yes	6	Administrative
New Hampshire	Yes	Yes	1,4,6	Administrative, Advisory
New Jersey	Yes	Yes	2	Administrative
New Mexico	Yes	No	2	Advisory
New York	Yes	Yes	1,2,3	Administrative, Policy
North Carolina	Yes	Yes	3	Administrative, Advisory
North Dakota	Yes	Yes	2	Administrative
Ohio	Yes	Yes	2	Administrative, Autonomous
Oklahoma	Yes	No	2,3	Advisory
Oregon	Yes	Yes	2,3	Autonomous, Advisory
Pennsylvania	Yes	Yes	1,3,4,5	Administrative, Policy, Advisory
Rhode Island	Yes	Yes	3,5	Policy
South Carolina	Yes	Yes	6	Policy
South Dakota	Yes	Yes	2	Administrative
Tennessee	Yes	Yes	3	Administrative
Texas	Yes	No	6	Advisory
Utah	Yes	Yes	6	Administrative, Policy, Advisory
Vermont	Yes	Somewhat	1,2,5	Administrative
Virginia	Yes	Yes	6	Administrative
Washington	Yes	Yes	2,6	Autonomous, Policy, Advisory
West Virginia	Yes	Yes	6	Administrative
Wisconsin	Yes	Yes	2	Administrative
Wyoming	Yes	Yes	6	Administrative

Note: Some respondents noted special exceptions to the choices offered.

TASKS TRUSTEES AND LIBRARIANS SHARE

Addressing operational concerns
Assessing literacy needs of the
    community
Attending all board meetings
Attending other meetings and
    workshops
Budgeting and financial
    management
Community involvement
Conducting a book sale
Conducting public relations
Cooperating for efficient library
    operation
Creating book selection policies
Creating new programs
Creating pleasant surroundings
Dealing with financial concerns
Determining library services
Fundraising
Keeping a competent librarian
Long-range planning
Maintaining grounds, lawn care,
    etc.
Making equipment purchases
Preparing agendas for monthly
    board meetings
Preparing annual reports
Promoting library use by
    community
Providing an ideal study
    environment
Providing resources for library
Purchasing equipment
Recruiting staff
Resolving conflicts
Reviewing policy
Revising the handbook
Securing gifts to library
Selecting books and materials
Setting library policy
Updating by-laws
Weeding books
Working at the library

states have a trustee manual, which usually has the answers to most of the questions.

CENTRAL KANSAS LIBRARY SYSTEM SURVEY OF TRUSTEES

One of the surveys I used was created by Timothy Lynch, who is currently with the Nebraska State Library Commission. The purpose of the survey was to determine how trustees and librarians perceived their own roles and those of their counterparts. It was sent to 350 trustees, primarily from libraries that serve less than 5,000 people.

Most trustees understand the major roles of trustees. A few trustees saw maintenance of the building, volunteering to work in the library, and listening to the librarian among their roles.

The following are some conclusions derived from the survey of CKLS Trustees:

- The smaller the library, the more willing trustees are to become involved in the day-to-day operations of the library.
- The smaller the library, the more willing trustees are to give instructions to staff members.
- The smaller the library, the more willing trustees are to have a higher profile in the management of the library.
- Trustees of larger libraries tend to have more formal education than trustees from smaller libraries.
- Trustees of smaller libraries tend to be older than trustees from larger libraries.
- Trustees from smaller libraries tend to have more frequent contacts with the librarians than do trustees from larger libraries.
- Ninety-three percent did not believe that fundraising was a basic responsibility of the library board of trustees.
- The smaller the library, the less willing trustees were to give even a modest gift of $25 to a major fundraising campaign.

SEE THINGS FROM BOTH SIDES

An important key to developing a good relationship between the librarian and the board is to see things from at least two perspectives—the librarian's and the trustees'. Every new board member presents a new challenge to the librarian. Here are a few concepts most librarians would like the trustee to know:

- Most public libraries are underfunded.

- Every library director feels caught in the middle between the board and the staff.
- Those who have responsibility for salaries are always under pressure to increase staff pay.
- Most library directors are committed to giving great library service free of charge.
- New board members don't usually know of the librarian's past accomplishments or the nature of the current working relationships.

Over the years a librarian will establish working guidelines based on the consensus or approval of the existing board. As the makeup of the board changes, new trustees may not be aware of old agreements and may question established patterns of conduct. They may even think the old ways are wrong and try to change them. All of a sudden the librarian has to defend behavior that has been acceptable in the past.

Change may be desirable, but it must come from the entire board. If you are a new board member, develop a sense of institutional history as soon as you can and learn the way things are, and why, before you try to change them. You could find yourself excluded from the center of influence if you try to change things too fast.

Trustees want their librarian to communicate better and keep them informed about happenings at the library, not just once a month at board meeting times, but during the month as important events occur. They want the librarian to take a greater interest in the orientation of new board members to help them learn the ropes more quickly. Some trustees want to become more involved in the day-to-day operation of the library, including book selection. This is almost invariably a mistake. Book selection is the librarian's job. Most trustees would rather leave the running of the library to the librarian.

MOST PRESSING PROBLEMS

When asked to name the most pressing problem faced by their libraries today, trustees responded with concerns about library policy, personnel conflicts, funding, adequacy and condition of the building, finding volunteers to serve on the board, and getting more people to use the library.

These problems are common among libraries. None of them are insurmountable, but there are no easy answers. They can probably be resolved if the librarian and board work together. The remaining chapters of *Working Together* deal with solving these problems by showing you how others have solved them and giving you tools to work through the problems yourself.

SUMMARY

Library directors and trustees have a unique opportunity to create a vision of service for their library. A sign in my office says, "My job is to give the people what they want when they come to the library." The realization of this vision requires the active cooperation of every board member and all the staff.

2 RECRUITING AND TRAINING TRUSTEES

Enthusiasm is the greatest asset in the world.
It beats money, power and influence.

Henry Chester

In 1980 the United State's Ice Hockey team defeated the Russian team for the Olympic Gold Medal. Some people thought we were just lucky. That may be true, but the coach, Herb Brooks, did as much as he could beforehand to get luck on his side. He started by looking for men who were willing to channel their egos for the success of the team. He used a psychological test to select his final players.

Having the right players is often the key to working together. If you can have some influence over selecting new members for your board, look for team players and suggest their names to those who make the final selection. Try completing a board member profile like the one following and giving it to city hall to give to prospective new board members:

Background Information for

Prospective Members of the

_____ *Library Board*

The purpose of the public library is to provide for educational, informational, and recreational needs of the people of the community and the surrounding area. It supports and encourages lifelong learning with special emphasis on educational activities for preschool children and out-of-school adults.

It is the goal of the library to give people what they want when they come to the library. The library does this by collecting and organizing materials in many formats so that people can find what they need. The library participates in a regional and statewide network so that materials not available locally can be borrowed from other libraries.

The library board is authorized by state law to operate the library [cite state code here] as a legal corporation, hire a qualified librarian, set library policy, and administer the library budget. The library is primarily funded by a tax on property within the city. Local funds are supplemented with state and federal funds, a system grant, gifts, and fines.

Major issues facing the board at this time are:

1. Increasing local funding in the face of property tax unrest.
2. Maintaining the building in good repair.
3. Providing enough books for people to read.
4. Having the library open the right hours to meet community needs.
5. [Add more of your own or substitute for the items above.]

At this time we are looking for new board members to replace _____ and _____, whose terms will expire April 30, 1993. We need someone with the following skills:

_____

Board members are expected to attend monthly board meetings which are held at _____ p.m. on the (fourth) (Thursday) [Fill in your own date and time.] of every month in the library. Board members are expected to be advocates for the library and work for its betterment. Occasional out-of-town trips may be requested. Rewards to board members are intangible, but nevertheless real. Board members benefit from being on the board by being involved in the management of an organization they care about.

Additional information is available by contacting:

(Board President) (Telephone).

(Adapted from: *Enhancing Board Effectiveness: Working with Boards, Councils, and Committees* by Barbara Bader and Steven Carr, Bozeman, Montana: Community Systems, 1989.)

No trustee is ever perfectly qualified when appointed for the first time. Good trustees qualify themselves as they serve. Effective trustee performance seems to be based on the following traits:

- Interest in the library, in the community, and the way each relates to the other
- Readiness to devote time and effort to the duties of library trusteeship
- Ability to establish impartial policies for the library
- High standards of personal conduct
- Willingness to allot sufficient time to prepare for and attend board meetings and other events
- Ability to work well with others

BALANCED REPRESENTATION FOR LIBRARY BOARD

- Artists
- Business people
- Children
- People of diverse racial, ethnic, and cultural backgrounds
- Government officials
- Grandparents
- Handicapped people
- Hobbyists
- Men and women of various ages and generations
- Parents
- Preschool oriented people
- Professionals
- Senior citizens
- Students
- Teachers

- Commitment to conducting library board business openly
- Ability to listen effectively
- Respect for the opinions of others.

Every new trustee has personal experience, skills, and talents that benefit the library. Common sense, clear-sighted political know-how, and leadership lead the list of valued assets you can bring to your board. But the most important qualification of all is an abiding interest in the library and its welfare.

In some small towns the main qualification for a library trustee is the willingness to say "yes." Trustees from some of the towns in central Kansas report they can't find enough willing people in town to serve on the library board. If this is your situation you may have to cultivate the interest of a few people and then educate them to the level you require in a trustee.

Guard against political cronyism on the library board. Often those who seek political appointments simply want higher political visibility, and are not team players. You don't need them on your board. Appointment to the library board must be nonpartisan. If board members come to board meetings representing any cause other than the good of the library, cooperative effort is in jeopardy.

Several years ago, a self-proclaimed religious mayor appointed a woman to my board who had demanded that the local school board remove some books from the school library. About two months after her appointment, she came to our library looking for books that had been the center of controversy in other libraries. She found three books that dealt explicitly with sex education. We had reserved the books to help parents teach their children. She checked out the books and took them to some ministers in town, asking them to bring a petition to have the books removed from the shelves. This set off a stir that has not been equaled since. For three months we spent all of our energies dealing with problems the board member had created. (The story is documented in "Bend but Don't Break" *Newsletter on Intellectual Freedom*, November 1981.) She finally resigned from the board, but not because of pressure from anyone.

Balanced representation should characterize the library board, but no one should "carry the flag" for a cause other than better library service to the entire community. For a variety of reasons, it is good to have both women and men on the library board, as well as representation from all community groups.

I do not recommend that the librarian get involved in the process of selecting new board members unless his or her participation is considered acceptable by members of the board and city officials.

Such involvement can appear to be manipulative and have repercussions later on.

NEW TRUSTEE ORIENTATION

Are you the newest trustee on your board? If not, you can probably remember when you were newly appointed. You were immediately expected to vote on issues, regardless of how qualified you felt. The information you are about to read could make a difference in the way a new library trustee performs his or her job and offer help in getting through the difficult time of beginning.

You may have lots of questions. Most new board members do. Write down your questions in a notebook as you read this next section. Then, when you have a chance, ask the librarian or another board member for the answers. Before you do that, you may want to ask yourself the following questions to help clarify your reasons for wanting to serve on the library board:

1. What was the first thing that started you thinking about becoming a library board member?
2. What are your feelings about the library?
3. What special skills do you have that might benefit the library?
4. Are you more concerned over taxes than you are about seeing the library grow?
5. Would you be willing to give a donation to the library to help with a building fund or special project?
6. Would you be willing to ask others to give to the library's building fund or some other project?
7. Is there something you would like to see changed about the library?
8. What is your real motivation for service on the library board?
9. How would you word a mission statement for the library?
10. Do you believe you understand the scope of good library service for all the people in your community?

Your job, right now, is to learn what you are supposed to do as a member of the library board. A good place to start is by reading your job description.

Sample Job Description

Job Title: Library Trustee

Accountable To: The taxpayers and the people served by the library.

Responsibilities: Responsible for working the board to oversee the general operation of the library, establish policy, determine the final budget, conduct public relations, and plan.

Duties: Attend all board meetings. Read board meeting minutes and other materials sent out before the board meeting. Become informed about all phases of library operation. Participate appropriately in board meetings. Serve on committees as assigned by board chair. Lend expertise and leadership to the board for the good of the library. Actively participate in systemwide workshops and activities. Participate in fundraising activities. Visit the library often and become acquainted with its services by using them.

Qualifications: A true sense of the library's enormous importance to the economic and social life of the community. Appreciation of library and a desire to provide the best possible service for the community. Sensitivity to the political conditions in the community.

Skills, Beliefs, Abilities: Ability to work with people. Ability to lead and preside at board meetings. Ability to plan. Belief in the importance of access to the materials of lifelong independent learning for everyone. Ability to communicate effectively.

LIBRARIAN: PROTECT YOUR TRUSTEES

Most library trustees have agreed to serve on the library board because they care about the library. Some may be unaware of the technicalities of the law and put themselves at risk inadvertently. One of your jobs is to help protect them from the risk of legal entanglements by omission. Areas of special concern include:

- Open meetings violations
- Conflicts of interest
- Non-management (failure to respond to clear needs to manage)
- Civil rights concerns in hiring
- Wrongful discharge

Eugene T. Hackler, an attorney from Olathe, Kansas, says, "The question of loyalty is one of conflict of interest, both of a personal nature and a corporate nature. Individuals should not profit as a result of their position on a board. Another agency should not benefit as a direct result of an individual's dual membership on the boards of both agencies. If a transaction occurs in which loyalties are confused, board members should vote against the transaction. Board members should ask this question as a good rule to follow: Would you be willing to have it publicly stated that your library is doing business with a board member? Check the specific laws in your state regarding conflict of interest to make sure your actions are in compliance.

"Attendance at board meetings is essential to avoid charges of non-management. If a board member cannot attend regularly, he or she should resign from the board. When an occasional meeting is missed, the board member should make sure to understand the minutes of that meeting. If the board member opposes any action made in his or her absence, then he or she should express that opposition in a letter to the secretary and request that the letter be placed with the minutes. It is not essential that board members dissent from each action that they would prefer to have gone the other way, but it is important on essential issues and particularly when those issues relate to the use of money or property of the library. The action to have the secretary record a dissenting vote can protect a board member, if the action taken by the rest of the board is ever questioned." (Hackler 1988.)

To Avoid Liability Exposure:

1. Don't jump to a conclusion. While reversible decisions can be made quickly, decisions that are nearly irreversible require more time.
2. Examine all the facts. Learn both sides of a disputed issue. Insist that staff provide you with complete and timely information before you act.
3. Know your institution's Articles of Incorporation, by-laws, internal rules, policies, and procedures as they are written down and follow them.
4. Use the available experts—the chief executive officer, president of the board, the board's attorney, accountant, and other paid professional advisors.
5. Perform your management duties. Remember that your duty is to the institution, not to any staff member.

6. Don't be a non-manager. Attend meetings and, if you miss occasionally, carefully read the minutes and register your disagreement by letter if you don't approve.
7. Avoid problems with dualities of interest.
   a. Disclose any dual loyalties.
   b. Don't debate or vote when you have a competing interest.
   c. Make sure there is a quorum present at the meeting, not counting yourself.

TRUSTEES: PROTECT YOURSELF

1. Review policies regularly, looking for personal exposure that might affect board members.
2. Ask a lawyer to review your policies for compliance with the law.
3. Have the library buy indemnity insurance for board members and the library director.
4. Be active in library affairs. Know what's going on. Attend all board meeting and vote "yes" or "no" on every issue.
5. Read the minutes carefully and make corrections.
6. Vote "no" if you don't have enough information.
7. Scrupulously avoid personal conflicts of interest and don't condone them in others.
8. Adhere strictly to the "open meetings law."
9. Don't do or say anything in a board meeting that could be construed to violate someone's civil rights.

Legal entanglements by trustees are rare. Most of them could have been avoided if trustees had been careful and knowledgeable.

EVALUATING THE BOARD

I believe that it is just as important for the board to evaluate itself as it is for it to evaluate the librarian. Here are a few questions that will help you focus on how well your board is doing:

1. Do we as a library board meet regularly and have a written agenda distributed in advance?
2. Do all of our board members attend the meetings regularly?

3. Does each member actively participate in the discussion and decisions?
4. As a board do we plan an orientation program for new members?
5. Has the library adopted a written statement of clear and specific objectives which serves as a basis of services and activities?
6. Is there a written policy manual?
7. Are the statements of objectives reviewed every year and revised if necessary?
8. Is our librarian included in board meetings and expected to present a monthly report to the board, either written or oral?
9. Does our board report regularly to the appropriating body and to the community with statistical, financial, and human interest facts?
10. Do members of the board and staff attend system and state library meetings?
11. Does the library provide funds to pay expenses of such meetings?
12. Are you familiar with the state statutes and city ordinances that govern your library operation?
13. Are you familiar with local library history?
14. If all the other trustees were to resign tomorrow, would you be prepared to take over, at least temporarily, as president?
15. When visiting another town, do you ever go to its library to look around?
16. Do you attend all meetings of the board?
17. Do you do your library homework?
18. Are you courteous to fellow trustees, even when you disagree with them?
19. Does the librarian, after gathering the appropriate information, meet with the board or a committee of the board to determine budget needs?
20. Is our budget estimate based on the current year's expenditures plus cost changes, expanded service, standards of good services, and the library's objectives?
21. Does the board formally adopt the budget at an official meeting before submitting it to the governing body?
22. Do members of the board participate in the presentation of the budget to the governing body?

23. Do you have a policy for accepting gifts, monetary as well as real property?
24. Are you taking full advantage of all existing funding programs—local, system, and state?
25. Is a systematic accounting of funds maintained by the librarian or someone delegated to this particular job?
26. Do all board members receive monthly financial statements that include the budget, current, and year-to-date expenditures with balances for each line item?
27. Do you have written, up-to-date job descriptions for all positions?
28. Are your salaries comparable to those paid in your community for comparable work, and also to the scale of other libraries of comparable size?
29. Does your staff have vacation and sick leave with pay, and an opportunity to participate in Social Security, retirement, and health insurance?
30. Does your staff have comfortable working conditions such as adequate light, heat, ventilation, and work and rest rooms?
31. Is your staff encouraged and helped to get in-service training through paid time and travel expenses to attend professional meetings and workshops?
32. Does your library service all parts of the community: geographic, economic, educational, occupational, social, retired, etc.?
33. Is the library dedicated to real service rather than to mere storage of books?
34. Does your collection meet the needs of the entire community?
35. Does the library take full advantage of the services offered by the library system?
36. Do you visit your library regularly?
37. Do you let your librarian administer the policies you make?

How did you do? Did the quiz give you a few things to work on with your librarian and other trustees? Now is a good time to start on the first one.

SUMMARY

Not everyone can be a good library trustee. Trustees have to be carefully selected, recruited, and trained to work together with others for the good of the people the library serves. Every board of trustees has an implicit responsibility to influence the selection of its board members—even if it is doing nothing more than preparing a copy of the Background Information sheet, in the first part of this chapter, and giving it to the mayor.

3 COMMUNICATING WITH EACH OTHER

Nature gave us one tongue and two ears
so we could hear twice as much as we speak.

Epictetus

Stephen Covey's fifth habit of highly effective people—Seek first to understand (then to be understood)—is the key to communication. Too many people get the process reversed. They are more worried about having their concerns understood than they are about understanding the concerns of others. While other people are talking, they are planning what they will say next. They would be much more effective at accomplishing their goal of being understood if they would practice active listening.

LISTENING SKILLS

Robert Bolton, in his book, *People Skills*, suggests four basic listening skills. They are:

- Offering reflective responses that provide a mirror to the speaker
- Paraphrasing
- Reflecting feelings
- Reflecting meaning

Active listening is demonstrated by asking questions, and rephrasing what others have said, until they agree that they have been understood. Then and only then does the active listener begin to explain his or her own viewpoint. This habit of communication is one of the master skills of life. It is the key to building win/win relationships and the essence of professionalism.

Here are some phrases you will hear from active listeners:

- "Let me see if I understand you. You are saying . . . "
- "In other words, I am hearing you say . . . "
- "Is this how you see it?"
- "Please help me to understand how you feel about the point you just made."
- "If I understand you correctly, you mean . . . "

We see the world as we are, not necessarily as it is. Our experiences lend much to our perceptions. Since none of us has the same life experiences, our perceptions will be different. Three people can experience the same event but, when asked to tell about it, will offer the questioner three different answers. If the questioner takes the time to practice active listening, he or she will probably get a more accurate account of the event.

Most credibility problems begin with perception differences; and perception is reality (to the other person). To resolve these differences and to restore credibility, one must seek first to understand the point of view of the other person. If you find yourself in a conflict situation because someone has misinterpreted what you said, try to understand the other person's point of view.

Communication, or the lack of it, causes more conflicts for librarians and board members than any other activity. Taking precipitous action based on our perceptions can exacerbate the conflict.

AVOID GIVING UNWANTED ADVICE

Sometimes people who consider themselves good listeners are quick to give advice. Your librarian may outline options for the board on how to solve a particular problem. Listening board members might ask questions for understanding, but they should never offer solutions suggesting action until the librarian has finished explaining all of the options. The librarian may not even want suggestions for solutions at this time. Whatever the situation, board members should not jump to an "action outburst." An action outburst sounds this: "Here's what you ought to do . . . " or "You should . . . " or "Why don't you . . . ?" If the person with the problem isn't ready for suggestions, action outbursts will tend to close down communication. Be sensitive to the situation and the person presenting the problem.

BASIS FOR CONFLICT

Conflict between two or more people occurs when the people are distressed about some important issues in their lives. They don't feel the way they want to feel. They feel a host of negative feelings including, loss, frustration, anger, lack of control, and emotional hurt. The key to resolving conflict is understanding the interest of the other person and finding out what it will take to get him or her to agree with you. The following process can help librarians and boards work through a conflict situation. It was developed by Elaine Yarbrough, a human relations consultant, and is used with her permission.

IDENTIFYING INTERESTS IN A CONFLICT

Elaine Yarbrough provides the following insight into interests in a conflict. "Most people begin a conflict with a *position,* which actually is a solution to a problem or concern they have. Then the parties to the conflict get deadlocked when they argue about whose solution to adopt, when the problem has yet to be identified. You may be engaged in a conflict about whether to undertake a certain program when you have not even discussed the problem you are trying to solve with the program.

"An interest is a desire, concern, goal, fear, or need. A position is something you have decided on; an interest is what caused you to decide.

"It is important to focus on interests because there are multiple ways of solving them and because there are similar interests that parties discover as they begin to explore their conflict. The similarities will draw them together and help prevent polarizing."

Ms. Yarborough's rules for identifying interests in a conflict follow:

1. *Ask the person,* "What are you concerned about? What is your goal? What problem are we trying to solve?"
2. Ask, "*What will it take* for you to cooperate with me?"
3. If you request something of another and get resistance, ask the other what prevents him or her from agreeing. You will need to take those objections into consideration as you seek a joint solution.
4. Notice the *triggering events* to a conflict. Often what happens prior to a conflict will give you clues about the underlying issues. For example, if a conflict erupts among the staff after every board meeting, the conflict may be about feelings toward the board and not about what's discussed among the staff.
5. Notice the *themes* in an interpersonal or group discussion. Themes can be picked up through the kinds of jokes and stories told, the kinds of images and metaphors that emerge, the topics that generate the most energy, or the ones that freeze the group. Sometimes risky conflict issues will emerge in these more indirect ways, and you can help clarify the concerns by verbalizing the theme.
6. Find out what change is specifically requested. Often, people will complain, give each other feedback, or attack without saying what they want the other to do. Making direct requests clarifies the conflict and often demonstrates that there is no conflict. For example, a janitor was complaining about all the extra work caused by community meetings in the schools. The community school director guessed that he wanted to stop cleaning

or to do it less well. However, when she asked him, the janitor said he wanted a new vacuum cleaner.

7. Listen and observe *nonverbals*, especially incongruent ones. If a person is saying pleasant words while frowning, you can guess that there are other issues in the conflict that have not yet been addressed.

8. Listen for *multiple interests*, some of which will be similar to yours, some of which will be different but not in conflict. Take multiple interests into account; they will help you to have flexibility in the conflict. You may not be able to give a person one thing he or she is asking for, but you can trade something else if you know more about the interests.

9. You may want to *keep a list* of interests so you can prioritize and remember them.

10. Meet the obvious needs, even it you suspect that there is something else underlying them. As you do so, the hidden interests will likely surface. For example, a committee chairwoman refused to bring flip charts to a meeting. They were too heavy, costly, and unaesthetic in members' homes. As the listener clarified these issues, what emerged was the chairwoman's need to be more important. She was tired of being the gopher.

11. Some indicators of position:

    "more of . . ."

    "less of . . ."

    "to get . . ."

    "to have . . ."

    We often want to solve problems by spending more money, hiring more people, or by reducing the number people, taking resources away. Or we'll say that our interest is to "have understanding" or that "no one understands me." Even though being understood is a fundamental human need, when people use that phrase in a conflict, the meaning is usually that if you understand me, then I'll get something. What I'll get is the interest.

12. To have clearly stated interests and agreements, we need to include how we'll know when we get there, the measure of the success. For example: "I want your respect. I will know I have it when you let me know you'll be late to meetings."

13. Sometimes the location of the discussion provides clues to the level of interest.

In summary, good agreements are:

- Specific
- Do-able
- Time-bound.

(Taken from *Identifying Interests in Conflict* by Elaine Yarbrough, © 1988 Yarbrough and Associates, 1113 Spruce, Boulder, CO, 80302. Quoted with permission.)

If you would like to work through a practice exercise in resolving conflict, see the Case Study in Appendix F. It presents a fictitious series of events which can be a powerful learning tool to help trustee and librarians develop skills to deal with conflict.

WHEN OFFENDED, TAKE THE INITIATIVE

Sometimes we are offended because of something someone says or does. Rather than harbor hurt feelings and act in an unseemly fashion towards the offending person, we can to take the initiative to resolve the disagreement. A direct approach to the person might be: "At our board meeting yesterday you said, ... Your comment bothered me a little, and I just wanted to see if I correctly understood what you said. (Covey's Fifth Habit) Did you mean . . . ?" The response will usually be: "I didn't mean that at all. This is what I meant." Or, "That was exactly what I meant, and I am sorry that you were offended by my remark." Or, "You understood me correctly. I didn't like what you said, and I wanted to let you know that I didn't appreciate it." Whatever the response, you have opened the channels of communication and created the opportunity to resolve differences.

If you decide to take the initiative when you have been offended, be careful not to offend the other person in the process. Confront the other person in the true spirit of wanting to understand, not vindictively or covertly seeking an apology. Describe your feelings and accept the negative aspect of the comment by saying: "I felt belittled . . . ," or "I felt embarrassed . . . ," rather than attacking the behavior with such labels as "childish" or "domineering." This preserves the dignity and self-respect of the other person, who then can respond and learn without feeling threatened.

THRESHOLD FOR AN APOLOGY

The opportunity to apologize or forgive someone is always

open. You could pick up the phone right now, call someone you have offended, and say, "I apologize." Or, if you have been hurt by them, "I forgive you." Doing so will give your an indescribable feeling of relief. You will re-open the lines of communications and create opportunities to work with the person in the future.

AVOIDING CONFLICT

Cooperative activities cannot survive amid conflict. A better way to avoid conflict is to stop it before it starts. Clearly defined channels of communication spell out relationships and expectations. If the board and the librarian seem unsure of their relationship to each other, it may help to develop formalized communication patterns. Several years ago, some staff members were unsure of their authority in the library. In response to their concern, I created a document entitled "Definition of Administrative Roles by Position " (Appendix E). It outlines various functions and activities in the library and defines the responsibilities of each position. The document has provided worthwhile guidelines for the staff and has helped trustees to understand my administrative style. You might use the document as a model to define the roles the library director and board members and staff.

BOARD MEETINGS

One of the few official opportunities for the board and the library director to get together and interact in a public way is at the board meeting. In no other forum are the lines of trustee roles and librarian responsibilities so clearly drawn yet, even when each knows his or her responsibility well, I have seen trustees acting like librarians in board meetings, and librarians acting like trustees in other meetings. Often it happens in the spirit of helpfulness and cooperation, but it also happens when one or the other usurps the authority of the other.

The board meets to transact business in public as a body corporate. The board approves the monthly expenditures and files the financial statement for the auditors. The board receives information from the library director and gives feedback on library activities. It adopts policy. It plans for program improvements. It approves personnel changes and adopts the final budget. The minutes of all board meetings are public documents and can be legally binding on the board.

The agenda of each board meeting formalizes the order of business. It is usually developed by the librarian and/or the chair of the board and should have a standard format. This should include roll call, the reading of the minutes and/or approval of the minutes if they have been mailed in advance of the meeting, and approval of the financial statement and of the monthly expenditures.

SPECIAL RULES FOR SMALL BOARDS

In an effort to make their board meetings a little less formal, some library boards have adopted "Procedures in Small Boards" from *Robert's Rules of Order*. It does not require a motion before an item can be discussed. No second is required for motions to come to the floor. It allows more flexibility for the board, yet it formalizes the procedure for the conduct of business.

Procedure in small boards. In a board meeting where there are not more than about a dozen members present, some of the formality that is necessary in a large assembly would hinder business. The rules governing such meetings are different from the rules that hold in assemblies, in the following respects:

- Members are not required to obtain the floor before making motions or speaking, which they can do while seated.
- Motions do not need to be seconded.
- There is no limit to the number of times a member can speak to a question, and motions to close or limit debate generally should not be entertained.
- Informal discussion of a subject is permitted while no motion is pending.

Sometimes, when a proposal is perfectly clear to all present, a vote can be taken without a motion's having been introduced. Unless agreed to by general consent, however, all proposed actions of a board must be approved by vote under the same rules as in other assemblies, except that a vote can be taken initially by a show of hands, which is often a better method in such meetings.

The chairman need not rise while putting questions to vote.

The chairman can speak in discussion without rising or leaving the chair; and, subject to rule or custom within the particular board (which should be uniformly followed regardless of how many members are present), he usually can make motions and usually votes on all questions." (Robert 1990, 477-78)

MAKING DECISIONS IN THE BOARD MEETING

Decisions are a regular part of board meetings. Although a consensus often occurs, occasional differences do surface. Sometimes those who hold different opinions cannot be persuaded to revise their point of view, though every effort should be made to reach a decision that all members can live with. Don't expect unanimity on all issues. After all, you would not want your board to be called a "rubber stamp" board. Encourage dissenting opinion as a source of new ideas.

Board decisions are often choices between two "competing goods." Here are four rules for identifying and setting priorities:

1. Pick the future rather than the past.
2. Focus on opportunity rather than on problems.
3. Choose your own direction rather than climb on the band wagon.
4. Aim for a decision that will make a difference rather than take the safe and easy route.

PROBLEM SOLVING

Board meeting are often the forum for solving library problems. Diagnosis is the first step toward solving a problem. State the problem precisely and defer consideration of solutions until later. Discussing solutions before the problem has been clearly defined only confuses the issue and slows the decision making process. Look for the component parts of the problem and then analyze the parts for specific causes.

It is the board chair's job to involve each member of the board in the discussion. Those who participate in the discussion are more likely to work to see the solution succeed. When discussing people connected with problems, it is wise to keep comments as positive as possible. The use of job titles rather than names will tend to keep the discussion impersonal. Avoid the personal pronoun "I." Using phrases like "Perhaps the board feels . . ." rather than "I feel . . ." can create a sense of unity rather than expose individual differences. Complaining about a problem serves no good purpose, while using positive suggestions like "This can be improved by . . ." can lead to a good solution.

Always be kind. Kindness will smooth over many ruffled feathers and move the process along.

Criticizing a member's contribution is a sure way to end con-

---

FIGURE 3-1 Sample Agenda

Meeting of the library board of the

Central Public Library

May 25, 1987

5:30 p.m.

Meeting Room of the Library

Presiding: Jeannette Derr, President

5:30 p.m.   Call to order

Roll call (Taken silently by the recording secretary)

Approval of minutes as written and sent to board members

Financial report

Approval of expenditures

Librarian's report	Courtney Crockett
Committee report: policy review	Barry Porter
Unfinished business	
Policy revision	Policy committee
Roof inspection	Leo Radenberg

New business

     Citizens request to reconsider a book

Other business

Adjournment.

structive communication. It is better to listen to everyone's comments without interrupting. Each person should have ample time to speak. When it is time to talk about solutions, a task-oriented discussion produces better results than a people-centered one, which can become involved in interpersonal conflicts. Identifying multiple solutions creates a greater potential for success. Don't evaluate specific alternatives until all of them have been considered.

When it is time to make a decision, evaluate all options. Then decide on an action plan that includes responsibility for each step and a timetable to follow. Write down the action plan with its steps and set a target date for the completion of each component. Follow up periodically on the implementation. The board should receive a report each month until the problem-solving action is completed.

DEALING WITH CONTROLLING INDIVIDUALS

The library board meeting should not be controlled by any one individual. When this happens, working together is impossible and meaningful communication ceases. The best solution to the problem is the direct approach, if it can be done without offending the person who dominates. Someone from the board needs to engage the controlling person in a private conversation and discuss the behavior. Some controlling people cannot accept negative feedback about themselves; others don't realize they are doing it. Either way, you have an obligation to the library to point out the behavior to the person involved and ask him or her to allow others more of an opportunity to participate.

THE BOARD MEETING AS A STAGE

As you become acquainted with members of the board, you will begin to perceive "an assortment of characters"—perhaps along these lines:

- *Expediters:* They want to see the meeting move along. They make the perfunctory motions to get to the next item of business.
- *Fiscal Beagles:* They ask questions about the budget and the expenditures.
- *Chair Warmers:* They rarely speak or offer suggestions.
- *Team Players:* They are genuinely interested in working together for the benefit of the library. They read all of the material. They ask informed questions and offer positive suggestions.

- *Parliamentarians:* They make sure Robert's Rules of Order are followed. Every board needs one.
- *Walking Encyclopedias:* They have opinions on everything that has happened in the past 50 years.
- *Information Dispensers:* It is usually the librarian who keeps board members current on library happenings.

When you understand the various parts, you can use the roles people have assumed to the advantage of the library.

DON'T WASTE TIME ON THE TRIVIAL

Most trustees are not paid for their service to the library. Their time is valuable. Don't waste trustees' time in discussing things that can or should be handled by the librarian. I went to a board meeting once where trustees discussed the relative merits of subscribing to *Time Magazine* for 20 minutes. The board should never take up board meeting time to handle business that is normally the duty of the librarian.

SUMMARY

Good communication is essential to working together. The better we understand and implement active listening, conflict resolution, and group decision techniques, the better our chances for accomplishing something great for our library are.

Librarians and trustees need to understand the dynamics of board meetings and their importance in the management of the library. Good board meetings don't just happen; they take work. Jointly, the librarian and the board president should develop the agenda and prepare to discuss each item.

4 HIRING A LIBRARIAN

Common sense is not so common.

Voltaire

Every vacancy is an opportunity for growth. Hiring a new librarian is like building a new library. A building should meet the needs of the community for the next 20 years. So should a new librarian; after all she or he may be there that long. The hiring decision should include such concepts as the potential for conceiving and implementing change and the ability to respond to the changing needs of the community. If the board hires a new librarian just like the old one, they are hiring status quo. Growth will not occur.

Try to anticipate the future, as much as possible. Several years ago, when we had a vacancy in the circulation department, we were just beginning to use microcomputers for overdue notices. It was natural to look for someone with a little computer experience. We hired a young man who had taken several computer classes and was interested in learning more. That decision changed the course of computer use in the library. It wasn't long until his job title changed to Automation Specialist. He became responsible for all computer decisions in the Central Kansas Library System and the Great Bend Public Library.

The hiring process starts with a vacancy, which is nothing more or less than a problem an employer will pay someone to solve. It is the board's job to define the need and find someone with appropriate skills to solve the problem. If you think of the process in these terms, it becomes less formidable.

SEARCHING

If you are serious about the opportunity for change the vacancy gives you, take time reflect on your library. It might be appropriate for the president of the board to appoint a search committee to find a new librarian. Whoever conducts the search should ask some soul-searching questions about the library, its programs and its future. The following worksheet lists a few questions to help you get started. The questions were designed to make you think about the opportunity/problem of hiring a new librarian. You may have other questions to stimulate the thinking of other board members.

MATCHING THE PERSON TO THE JOB

Every hiring decision should be a matter of matching the person to the job. The first step is to define the job. If you don't you have a job description for the position of library director, now may be a good time to write one. One caution about job descriptions: they are often written by the person who is currently in the job and typically describe that person's responsibilities at the time of the writing. Create the job description by reviewing the job requirements and define them in terms of the following:

- Administrative: Will the librarian be running the library with very little help from the board? Or will it be a team effort?
- Personnel/Supervisory: How many people, if any, will the librarian supervise?
- Policy/Decision-Making: Will the librarian make recommendations to the board for policy? What decisions will be delegated?
- Planning/Organization: Will the librarian be required to formulate plans and organize for implementation?
- Speaking/Writing: What communication skills are required? Will the librarian be writing news releases or giving speeches to community groups?
- Evaluative: Will the librarian be required to process information, review alternatives, and evaluate results? What about book selection?
- Diagnostic: Will the librarian be required to recognize problems and make recommendations to the board for solving them?

The following job description may be useful as a guide:.

Sample Job Description

Job Title: Librarian

Supervised by: Library Board

Responsibilities: Responsible for general library operation, supervision of staff, and service to the public. Cooperates as a link with staff and library board to achieve efficient library operation.

Duties: Attends all board meetings and serves as advisor to the board on all matters. Responsible in all areas of library management, including personnel supervision, budget prepa-

FIGURE 4-1 Worksheet for Hiring a Librarian

1. What is the library's image in the community?

2. Does the image need sprucing up, developing, or expanding?

3. What would you like it to be ten years from today?

4. What are the major problems a new library director will face and be expected to solve during the first two **months** on the job?

5. What are the major problems a new library director will face and be expected to solve during the first two **years** on the job?

6. What is the board's role in solving these problems?

7. What specific activities would you expect the librarian to implement to solve these problems?

8. What was the leadership style of the former librarian?

9. Was his or her leadership style effective with the current staff?

10. Was his or her leadership style effective with the board?

11. What leadership qualities do you think will work best with the staff? With the board?

ration, acquisitions, programming, and training. Supervises staff, makes general task assignments, schedules work hours and vacation, trains new staff members, and maintains atmosphere of cooperation and good feeling. Selects library materials according to the library's book selection policy. Selects materials to be discarded from collection. Works with board on preparation of budget. Recommends salary increases for staff members. Implements library programs, policies, and objectives as established by the board. Attends meetings of state and national professional association. Creates plans to extend library services to everyone in the community.

Qualifications: M.L.S. degree from an ALA-accredited university; several years experience as a professional in a public library.

Skills and Abilities: Thorough knowledge of all phases of public library operations. Ability to supervise staff. Above-average decision-making skills. Ability to communicate orally and in writing.

If you have a job description for the library director, get it out of the file and review it. Ask yourself a few questions:

1. Does the job description focus on detailed tasks rather than on a few general administrative responsibilities?
2. Does the job description contain "excess baggage" that looks more like a wish list created by a committee?
3. Do the qualifications expected for the position match the salary, or is the job description filled with unrealistic expectations?
4. Could the job description become the basis for a performance appraisal instrument?
5. Is the job description flexible enough to allow someone new to capitalize on individual strengths he or she might bring to the job?

With the answers to these questions, rewrite the job description and use it to help match the person to the job. This should take care of the objective part of the procedure, but what do you do about the subjective part of the selection process? What about aspects of the candidate such as character and personality? How do you measure such qualities? You set the standard, devise the questions, and observe the behavior in the interview. The form in Figure 4-2 may help.

You may have other ideas for such a chart. Make a copy of the blank chart and fill it in with your own list. It is your problem/opportunity, and the board has the right to determine the job qualifications. Be prepared to justify what you do. Remember that you are looking for the person who best matches your job requirements and that the decision could come down to very subjective points.

FINDING APPLICANTS

Once you have defined the job, it is time to seek applicants. Here again, the board has a wide range of options. If your are looking for someone with a Master's degree in library science plus several years of experience, a national search may be necessary. A "Positions Open" advertisement in *Library Hotline, Library Journal, American Libraries,* or *Wilson Library Bulletin* will put you in touch with several qualified applicants. An ad will cost $50 to $300 and up per issue, depending on its length.

The main purpose of advertising for the position is to obtain a significant pool of applicants. If you are looking for someone without a Master's degree, you can probably find enough qualified job seekers by using a local newspaper with wide circulation. Ideally, you would like to have 20 or more qualified applicants. Some of my worst hiring decisions were made by hiring from too small an applicant pool. If you have only one applicant and you hire him or her, you may never know if there was someone better just around the corner.

To attract a good applicant pool, it is important to write a good job advertisement. You want your ad to help potential applicants to screen themselves. For example, a job listing for a library clerk might read like this: *"Help wanted—Circulation clerk for the library. Apply in person, 212 N. Main."* You will probably have more applications than you can deal with. On the other hand if you include "must be able to type" you will eliminate about half of the potential applicants. Listing skills and educational level, and the job's hours and salary, will cause others to pass over your job. That's what you want.

It is better to spend more money for a larger ad and let potential candidates eliminate themselves than to spend less for a short ad and spend extra time with applications submitted by people who do not qualify. Here are some tips for writing the ad:

- Give the job title
- Describe the job in ten words or less (refer to the job description)

FIGURE 4-2 Subjective Traits Evaluation Form

In addition to comments, rank on a scale of 1 to 10

Trait	Desired Behaviors	Candidate_____
Personality	Easygoing, pleasant, and able to relate to almost everyone. Cool under pressure.	
Character	Honest, fair, free of prejudice.	
Appearance	Neat, well-groomed, appropriately dressed.	
Attitude	Positive, self-confident, refrains from finding fault or blaming others.	
Motivation	Self-directed, goal-oriented, has a vision for the future.	
Enthusiasm	Eager to serve others, able to involve others in his or her personal vision.	
Leadership	Flexible, open to new ideas, supportive of others.	
Manners	Observes social norms, sensitive to others.	

FIGURE 4-2 *Cont'd.*

In addition to comments, rank on a scale of 1 to 10

Trait	Desired Behaviors	Candidate_____

- List the responsibilities and job requirements
- List the individual qualifications
- State the hours
- Specify the salary in a flexible way: "Negotiable from $___" (Ads in *American Libraries* require a salary statement)
- Tell how to apply
- State the application deadline
- Be specific

Remember that in advertising for a position you must avoid references to age, sex, religion, race, national origin, or disability, because such references can be considered discriminatory. You may, however, include a bona fide occupational qualification (BFOQ) that may or may not exclude representatives from one of the protected groups. The requirement to work on Saturday may discriminate against those who attend religious activities on Saturday, but if the library is open on Saturday and everyone who works for the library is required to work on Saturday, you have the right, even the obligation, to include the information in the job ad or on the application.

The final test for discrimination can be summed up in these three questions:

- Are we consistent?
- Do we have a reason?
- Is it documented?

If the answer is "yes" to all three questions, you are probably on safe ground.

READING THE RESUME

A resume is a good way to receive preliminary information about prospective employees, though the information may paint a "bigger-than-life" picture of the person. Richard W. Meyer in "How to Read an Applicant Resume" (Meyer 1987) gives a neat outline on reading a resume:

Presentation
- Quality of presentation: Neat, error-free appearance
- Writing skill: Articulate and straightforward
- Organization: Logical order, starting with name and address
- Pertinence: Information relevant to the position

Experience
- Cumulations: New assignments built on prior learning experiences
- Progress: Growth resulting from progressively responsible positions
- Learning: New programs developed show management confidence
- Leadership: Demonstrated ability to organize and implement new programs

References
- Who they are: Are they from current or former supervisors or friends?
- What they say: Do they indicate positive contributions made by applicant?
- What they don't say: Do they avoid commenting on specific questions you are concerned about?

THE APPLICATION FORM

A resume may give you good information about the applicant, but it doesn't answer some of the questions that may be on the application. Never accept a resume instead of a completed application. If you conduct a local search, it is all right to ask people to come to the library to fill out an application. With a national search you usually ask candidates to send a resume. When they do, you return a blank application form along with other information about the library and the job, including a job description.

As in all other phases of the process, the application must not ask questions that could allow the evaluators to discriminate against protected groups. Following is a sample that our library has been using. We have tried to eliminate discriminatory language or questions. This application is set up on a computer so that we can customize it for each vacancy. I would discourage you from using more than two pages.

The application will help you discover reasons to continue considering the applicant. Look at past accomplishments as a predictor of performance in your library. For example, someone who couldn't get along with others in a former job may have problems getting along with a supervisor in your library.

After looking at the educational achievements and related work experience, I look at "reasons for leaving." The words "fired" and "quit" send up a red flag to me. The best reason for leaving is "to take a better job." The answer suggests that the applicant is working to better himself or herself. Another significant question

APPLICATION FOR EMPLOYMENT

TO APPLICANT: *Federal and State Laws require that all applications be considered without regard to race, religion, color, sex, age or national origin.*

PERSONAL   (Please Print)   Date _____

Name _____ Social Security No. _____
      Last   First   Middle

Present Address _____
      No.   Street   City   State   Zip

Telephone Number_____ How long have you lived at present address?_____

Previous Address _____ How long?_____
      No.   Street   City   State

Position(s) applied for _____ ☐ Full time   ☐ Part time

If part time specify days/hours_____ Rate of pay expected $ _____ per_____

Have you worked for us before?_____ If YES, when? _____

List any relatives/friends working for us_____

Indicate special qualifications or skills_____

_____

EDUCATION Name and Location of School	Course of Study	No. of Years Completed	Did You Graduate?	Degree
ELEMENTARY				
HIGH SCHOOL				
COLLEGE				
OTHER (Specify)				

PRIOR EMPLOYMENT (Name and Address)
List name of supervisor for each position.
Check box next to employer's name indicating those you do not wish us to contact.

Name and Address	Period From To	Job	Salary Start Final	Reason for Leaving
☐				
☐				
☐				
☐				

PERSONAL REFERENCES Name and Address (Not former employers or relatives)	Telephone

SUPPLEMENTAL QUESTIONS

1. Do you have a legal right to work in the United States?   Yes _____ No _____

2. Have you ever been convicted of a felony? Yes _____ No _____ If yes, explain.

3. Have you ever been disciplined or fired?   Yes _____ No _____ If yes, explain.

3. Can you type? Yes _____ No _____ Number of words per minute? _____

5. List any reason known to you why you might be unable to perform consistently and promptly the duties of the job.

6. What did you like best about your most recent job?

7. What did you like least about your most recent job?

8. Describe your supervisory experience

9. Describe your library experience in working with adults, young adults and children.

10. Check each space and sign below:

    ——— I hereby authorize theLibrary to contact prior employers to obtain any and all informationrelated to my work performance.

    ——— The information provided by me in this application is true and complete to the best of my knowledge. I understand that if I am employed, any false statement will be considered as cause for possible dismissal.

    ——— I have read the job description for the advertised position and know of no reason I cannot perform the tasks as outlined.

    Signature of Applicant _____ Date _____

DO NOT WRITE BELOW THIS LINE

INTERVIEW AND HIRE INFORMATION

Interview remarks _____

_____

HIRED _____ DATE _____ JOB TITLE _____

STEP _____ CLASS _____ PAYSCALE _____ PERHOUR _____

FULL-TIME _____ PART-TIME _____ PART-TIME HOURLY _____ HOURS PER WEEK _____

_____   _____
Signature of Interviewer   Signature of Director

is, "What did you like least about your most recent job?" Whatever the applicant says can be transferred to your job. If the working conditions were a problem there, they might be a problem at your place too. In the interview you can explore these questions in greater detail. Remember, the application form is just one more screening device to help you select the person who best matches your job requirements.

INTERVIEWING

ALA PLACEMENT SERVICE
One of the best opportunities for employers and job seekers occurs at the mid-winter and the annual conferences of the American Library Association. The Office of Personnel Relations does a great job of bringing applicants and employers together for face-to-face interviews. Their placement service provides a clearing house of available positions for job seekers, and of prospective applicants for employers. Each job seeker or employer fills out a one-page form which is duplicated and placed in looseleaf notebooks by job classification—administration, reference, technical services, etc. Employers and job seekers send messages to each other on a standardized form using an identification number. Employers reserve tables in the interview area and set up preliminary interviews with applicants.

You should take copies of your library's job description, blank application forms and some information about your library and town with you to the interview. In the interview you will want to exchange information with the candidate; allowing about half of the time for the candidates to answer questions and talk about themselves and the remaining time for you to talk about the job and answer questions from the applicants.

AFTER THE SCREENING INTERVIEW
You want the best candidates to come to your town and see your library before offering someone the job. Your chances of finding several people to invite in for an interview are very good. A drawback to using the ALA Placement Service is the expense of travel for both the library trustees and the applicants. Another drawback is timing. ALA Conferences are held in January and June and you may not be able to wait for the next conference to hire a

new librarian. I would recommend a diversified approach, such as ads in national journals and one or more of the joblines offered by state library associations. See *American Libraries* for a list of available joblines.

Once you have reviewed the completed applications and narrowed the list to three or four, it is time to set up on-site interviews. If the applicants don't have to travel very far, you may want to interview more than four. If you have conducted a national search, you have to decide how to conduct the interviews. You may want to conduct telephone interviews to narrow the field for on-site interviews. Most libraries have limited resources to pay for interviews. So do the candidates. The library should pay the travel expense for the interviews. You could miss some excellent candidates if you don't.

FINAL INTERVIEWING

Once you have reviewed the all of the written material submitted by the candidates and have selected those you want to interview, it is time to work with other board members to determine the questions you are going to ask. I have two cautions regarding the questions to be asked in an interview: 1) Ask only those questions that pertain to the candidate's past or potential job performance; 2) Don't allow others involved in the process put the board at risk by asking illegal questions.

Beforehand, review the plan for the interview with your board, perhaps during an executive session of a regularly called meeting. Make a list of the questions you plan to ask, and ask all interviewees the same questions. Following are some questions:

- Tell us about yourself.
- What were the circumstances concerning your leaving your last job?
- Please expand upon those aspects of your school (or last job) which you found most satisfying.
- What experiences have you had with _____ (personnel supervision, book selection, working with boards or government officials)?
- Why do you think this library should hire you?
- What are some things you wish to avoid in the next job?
- What did you like best about your last job?
- Do you consider yourself a self starter? Why?
- What did you like least about your last job?
- What would you do if your supervisor (the Board) made a decision with which you strongly disagree?

The Alexander Hamilton Institute (197 West Spring Valley Ave., Maywood, NJ 07607) has published a pamphlet entitled, *Interviewing Made Easy: The Right Way to Ask Hiring Questions.* It includes a quiz to see how your how your hiring savvy stacks up against the finer points of interview questions. The quiz is followed by 39 ready-to-use questions based on common job requirements found in many job descriptions.

STAFF INVOLVEMENT

In today's atmosphere of participatory management, it is important that staff members feel that they have participated in the selection process. But it is a delicate matter. If staff members are given too much control in the process, they may feel they can control the situation after the hiring decision is made. This could undermine the authority of the new director. If the board ignores the staff in the hiring process, staff members could make things difficult for the new director, who will have to work with both the staff and the board.

SITUATION QUESTIONS

When you are trying to determine how the person will perform in the position of library director, situation questions are often helpful. You give the candidate a dilemma that could occur in your library and ask how he or she would respond. You are looking for problem solving and management skills. Please remember that they don't have to agree with you to be right for the job. Their answer may be better than yours. You have to allow for creative differences.

The City of El Paso, Texas, has a personnel department that conducts interviews for city department head positions; the library board is advisory. Dick L. Moody, Recruitment and Examination Analyst, shared their employment process for the position of Library Director:

1. We advertise the minimum qualification, salary range, and examination place in various local, regional, and national periodicals for 60 to 90 days.
2. We screen the applications on the basis of the minimum qualifications concerning education and/or experience.
3. If we receive a large number of qualified applicants, we administer a written examination and invite the top eight to an assessment center examination.
4. In preparation for the assessment center, we develop several job-related exercises to simulate the requirements of the

job. For example, we frequently develop an in-basket exercise made up of the types of letters, memos, and phone messages that must be handled by one in that position. We devise a role-play scenario for each candidate to act out in front of the assessors. We devise a group problem-solving exercise in which the candidates either compete with one another in a hypothetical situation where not everyone will be granted approval or the needed resources for reaching a goal, or will collaborate in developing a recommendation for a superior.

During the one or two days of the assessment center, each candidate is viewed and interviewed by each assessor. At the end, the assessors are required to reach a consensus on a set of rating factors for each candidate.

The candidates are then put in rank order on the basis of their ratings. Those who do not reach the pre-announced minimum score are not included on the list of eligibles for the position.

5. The hiring official, who is briefing the assessors, plays no part in the assessment center, but selects the top three on the list to fill the position after each of the three has been given a hiring interview.

Throughout the process of taking applications and conducting interviews, you are looking for information that indicates, "This person does not match our job requirements." Let's hope that at least one person makes it through the test with flying colors. If not, it may be better to search for another group of applications and look for a new batch of people than to settle for someone whom you don't believe to be fully qualified.

DECIDING

After you complete the process, the final decision may come down to a question of feelings. If the whole board feels good about the person you decide to hire, you are probably making the right choice. Remember, there is no one perfect person for every job vacancy. Several different people could fill the vacancy equally well.

When I think of the hiring decisions I have made, the choices that didn't work out well were those I had doubts about even as I made the decision. After all you do to make the selection process objective, sometimes the best question of all is: "Do we feel good about the person we have selected?"

You may want to use this final checklist of questions before hiring a new library director:

HIRING CHECKLIST

1. Do we have a clear idea of what the job requirements are?
2. Does the person we have tentatively selected match these job requirements better than any of the other candidates?
3. What is the most important qualification for this job?
4. What are the skills or qualifications of the person we have tentatively selected that match this most important requirement?
5. What are the major strengths of the candidate we have selected?
6. Does everyone on the board feel good about the person we have selected?

DECIDING ON PERQUISITES

Before you make the hiring decision you must make decisions about staff perquisites.

Here is a list of questions you should have in mind when you make the offer.

1. What is the salary range for this position? What is the maximum salary you will offer anyone regardless of the qualifications?
2. What are the health insurance benefits? Are they different from those of other staff members?
3. How much vacation will the library director receive?
4. What is the sick leave policy?
5. Are there other perquisites that go with the position, such as the use of a vehicle or disability insurance?
6. What constitutes a normal work week? Will the director be expected to work nights or weekends?
7. When will the new director start work?
8. How much, if any, of the moving expenses will the library pay?

Many of these items are negotiable. Others are defined in library policy. All of these issues should be detailed in the confirming letter to the person you hire.

EXPECT THE BEST AND EXPECT TO PAY FOR IT

When it comes to negotiating monetary considerations, he library board should be generous rather than stingy. After all, you are hiring someone to solve the problems of running your library and to do so satisfactorily.

In a South Sea folktale Johnny Lingo goes to his prospective father-in-law to bargain for the hand of Mahana in marriage. Some islanders wonder if she will fetch even two cows because she is so ugly. Imagine the surprise of all the islanders when Johnny offers eight cows—more than any man has ever paid for a wife. Mahana becomes the most beautiful woman on the island, because her husband knew enough about self-worth to elevate her status by giving eight cows for her.

Why cheapen the value of your new director by quibbling over money? I'll never forget the comment of one of the board members who hired me to direct the Central Kansas Library System and the Great Bend Public Library. We had already agreed on salary and were talking about fringe benefits. Peg Woods said, "After we have bought the elephant, why quibble over peanuts?" The rest of the negotiations went smoothly. I will always be grateful to her for saying that. Her comment set the tone for working with that board for years to come.

Of course, if you don't have the flexibility to offer one cent more than the advertised salary, offer the stated salary and don't apologize. You can add value to the job in other ways. The desired outcome is for both the library board and the new library director is to feel good about the hiring decision.

MAKING THE OFFER

When you are ready to offer the job to someone, call and make the offer. If he or she accepts, follow the verbal offer with a written confirmation in duplicate. Ask the person to sign the agreement and return one copy. There may be compelling reasons for wanting to finalize the deal while the person is still in town. If everyone agrees, go ahead. Notify the unsuccessful candidates that the position has been filled, once the new librarian is on the job.

"Information for New Employees" (Appendix D) is a sample of the kind of document you should have for every new employee, including the librarian. It answers questions new employees are sure to ask. You can add or subtract ideas as they pertain to your library.

SUMMARY

The opportunity to hire a new librarian may be the best chance you will ever have to improve your library. Your hiring decision will have an impact on your library and your community for years to come. Do it right and don't put yourself or your board at risk by doing or saying something that will expose you to discrimination charges. Review the federal and state laws. Make sure that everyone on your board knows them. You may want to seek the advice of an attorney or get some help from an executive search firm.

5 WORKING WITH THE LIBRARIAN

When we talk about other people,
we say as much about ourselves as we say about them.

James Swan

Dear Library Board Member,

I love my job and really appreciate the opportunity to serve the public each day. Each day is an exciting challenge with no two days alike. However, the events of the past two months have prompted me to express my feelings.

I wish to commend the board members for their hard work and effort they put into their decisions made during recent executive sessions.

In order to function well, the librarian and library board need to work together. Although I have felt this has been the case until now, there are several places I feel communication has broken down:

1. I did not receive an advance copy of the changes before the board meeting.
2. I never received a written copy of the changes decided in executive session and still do not have one.
3. My input was never asked on any of the changes before a vote was taken.
4. Changes affecting hours for the staff were never discussed with the staff.

While I feel that many of these changes are excellent and should be tried, I feel upset because I was never consulted.

I would hope future changes made by the board would be decided as a joint effort so that, working together, we can provide the best service possible. Let us work toward open communication.

Working together we can accomplish great things and meet the needs of each library patron.

Your Librarian

OPEN COMMUNICATION

The preceding letter was written by a librarian. What was she saying about herself? What was she saying about her board? It is filled with clues that the librarian and the board are not working together. The most obvious one is the lack of communication. The board has held special sessions because they want the librarian to make some changes they felt would improve the library. The librarian is threatened by these meetings. I attended the board meeting where these concerns were aired, and I am confident that the librarian and the board wanted the same thing for the library—they wanted people to get what they want when they go to the library.

I was in this same library more than a decade ago when the board hired this librarian. The people who were there then have long since rotated off the board. New board members have replaced them and have come to expect new things from the librarian. I have seen more librarian/trustee relationships fail because of poor communication than any other single factor. The question is: "How can the library board effect change in the library without threatening the librarian." The answer is communication—open and constant—between the librarian and the board.

Decisions made by the board in executive session are threatening to the librarian, if not illegal. Board decisions made without the input of the librarian can imply that the librarian is not doing a good job. In this case, the board agreed that the librarian was doing a good job, but felt that the library's service could be improved. The preferred way to bring about change is to open the lines of communication and reason together.

ORIENTATION

Once you have hired your new librarian, it is time to begin the orientation process. This phase is critical to your director's success and your ability to work together. Make sure that she or he gets acquainted in the community by meeting all segments of its power structure. The success of your library depends on your new librarian's ability to work with the people in the community, so do yourself and the librarian a favor—help your librarian to get off to a good start.

The library director's relationship with the staff is his or her responsibility. The board should not interfere. But you might encourage a staff meeting and perhaps an interview with everyone if the staff isn't too large.

Be ready for the changes the librarian wants to make. Your job as a library trustee is to see that the library runs smoothly, that the people who use the library get what they need. You have hired a librarian to meet that challenge for you. Get out of the way and let it happen with your full support. Simply make sure that the lines of communication stay open.

PERFORMANCE APPRAISAL

Performance appraisal is a systematic evaluation of the employee's performance and potential. As defined in "Performance Appraisals: The Latest Legal Nightmare," it includes a review of:

- The employee's current performance
- The employee's potential for career development
- Shortcomings to be corrected
- Training and experience needed to correct weak spots.

You can see that this definition includes more than the employee's current job performance. It is an overall evaluation that might be used in a variety of ways. Some of these could be helpful, while other parts might be threatening to the librarian.

I do not recommend formal performance appraisals because they create barriers to working together and because research on their efficacy is inconclusive. I much prefer an ongoing dialogue with the librarian, such as might occur during regular board meetings. The only value in a formal performance appraisal is for the library director is to hear the board speak with one voice about his or her performance. Regular conversations with the librarian will give better feedback and more help than one save-it-up-and-blast-the-librarian annual review. I have enjoyed a mini "performance appraisal" with board members every month. Some stop by my office or call me on the telephone just to touch base. Sometimes I initiate the call. Every visit you have with the librarian provides feedback and encouragement. Feedback and encouragement should be the only reasons for a performance appraisal, and these can be given and received in short meetings rather than one big meeting.

If your board insists on having an annual performance review, using a formalized document, make sure that the librarian is involved in the process of creating the document. The performance review form should be explicit and relate entirely to the job. Hidden agendas or uncommunicated expectations are not allowed. Following are 21 points that could serve as the basis of a performance review form:

LIBRARY DIRECTOR PERFORMANCE APPRAISAL

This document is drawn from the job description for the library director. It is designed to give board members the opportunity to evaluate the director on performances they have to opportunity to observe.

Use the following rating scale:
4 = Strongly Agree
3 = Agree
2 = Disagree
1 = Strongly Disagree

Make remarks in the "Comments Section" by referring to the numbered statement and following with the comment.

Budgeting and Financial Management

1. ____ The Director manages the library's resources appropriately.
2. ____ The Director involves board members appropriately in managing library resources.
3. ____ The Director prepares budgets and oversees preparation of financial statements so board members can understand them.

Communications

4. ____ The Director attends all board meetings and participates appropriately.
5. ____ The Director's reports and proposals to the board are well-written, containing enough information to help board members make informed decisions without being wordy or lacking in essential details.
6. ____ The Director's communications with board members outside board meetings are appropriate.
7. ____ The Director represents the library at important state, regional and national meetings and reports on significant happenings.
8. ____ The Director communicates appropriately with constituents, elected officials, and the public.

Policies and Guidelines

9. ____ The Director recommends policy changes as needed, with suggested wording.

10. ____ The Director implements board policy and guidelines appropriately.

Staff Recruiting and Supervision

11. ____ The Director keeps the board informed about staff changes.

12. ____ The Director does a good job of administering salaries, involving the board appropriately.

13. ____ The Director delegates responsibility and authority to staff members in a way that empowers them to do their jobs well and accomplish the mission of the library.

Staff Training

14. ____ The Director does a good job of preparing and presenting training opportunities for staff members and trustees.

15. ____ The Director attends appropriate continuing education opportunities.

Overall Administration

16. ____ The Director sets appropriate goals and works to accomplish them.

17. ____ The Director does an overall good job of administering the affairs of the library.

Comments Section.

If you have an additional comment about any of these statement, write the number of the comment and then your comment.

18. Noteworthy accomplishments of the Director during the past year have been:

19. Situations that might have been handled differently were:

Goal Setting

20. The following are goals the Executive Committee would like to see the Director accomplish during the next calendar year:

21. The following are the goals the Director would like to accomplish during the next calendar year:

GOAL SETTING

Of much more value than the performance appraisal is the process of setting goals and having a goal accountability session with the librarian. The board and librarian sit down together and together set some goals for the library. At the end of the year they review the goals that were set the year before. It is best to keep the list short and to ask the librarian to give quarterly or even monthly accountability reports. There should be no surprises. If you are unhappy with your librarian right now, pick up the telephone and call him or her. Set up a time to meet to discuss your concerns. Don't wait! Do it today.

If handled properly, performance review can be used to build the spirit of working together and improve morale and performance. The August 30, 1987 issue of *Supervisor's Bulletin* describes feedback interview developed by Ellen T. Ahearn. She suggests asking questions to encourage employees to discuss their jobs from their point of view. In a library setting, for example, the questions might be:

- How are things going at the library?
- What problems are you having meeting the needs of the patrons?
- Are the problems due to a lack of resources or staff training?

Ms. Ahearn also suggests avoiding defensiveness. "Even the most tactful supervisors sometimes ask a questions or make a statement that appears as criticism to the employee and puts him or her on the defensive," she says. Avoid negative, judgmental words that can ruin an interview, such as lousy, stupid, horrible, or idiotic. Direct the discussion toward the job and the employee. Summarize comments as the interview progresses. It shows you are listening; it reiterates points already covered; it increases understanding; it helps re-check and distill ideas; and it helps distinguish between covered topics and remaining points. Pause often to allow the librarian time to make remarks without feeling pressure. This feedback interview is less threatening than more formal appraisals to the employee and opens the channels of communication.

The American Library Trustee Association's publication *Evaluating the Library Director* by Nancy M. Bolt is well worth obtaining. Ms. Bolt says, "It is possible for the library director to have accomplished a great deal but to have alienated the staff, public, governing body, and the board as well. It is also possible for the library director to be well-liked and project an air of competent management, but in fact not accomplish progress toward stated or unstated goals and objectives for the development of the library.

"An evaluation of library management requires that the board and the director both agree on the meaning of good management. Meaningful measurement of results against expectations requires mutual agreement on what is to be accomplished."

You have to work together to develop a helpful process.

Ms. Bolt gives two reasons for evaluating the library director: "1) To determine how well the library is being managed, and 2) to measure the library director's accomplishments." Another reason to evaluate the director is to give the board the opportunity to speak with one voice, rather than have the librarian hear disparate comments from several board members.

ADVICE TO A NEW LIBRARIAN

It is important to remember that you cannot expect the new librarian to run the library the same way the former librarian did. Perhaps a good way for trustees to understand this change is to read my advice to a newly appointed librarian. The most difficult task for a librarian just starting a new job is getting the "lay of the land." Not only does the new librarian have to become familiar with the board members, but the staff is waiting to see what their new boss is going to do to them (or, as they hope, for them). Fortunately, there seems to be a "honeymoon" period for newly appointed librarians.

Many times a new director can take charge and make changes that a long-standing incumbent librarian can't. I remember a situation I had several years ago. When I discovered that several employees were earning less than the federal minimum wage, I went to the board and secured salary adjustments for them. The board gave me an unprecedented vote of confidence. It was a good move and sent a clear message to the staff.

"Never make changes faster than your authority to do so is recognized." Dr. M. P. Marchant, a friend and professor of library science at Brigham Young University, gave me this sound piece of advice when I graduated from library school. In other words be sure of your own authority on several fronts before introducing change. If you are going to recommend raises for everyone, make sure the board is with you before you stick your neck out. If you plan to change the hours of the library, be sure the staff will support the changes and that the public will consider your new hours as an improvement in service.

MAKE A "TO-DO" LIST

Before your first day on the job, create a to-do list. Here is one I recommend:

1. *Interview every staff member, if possible.* Perhaps they could fill out a one-page, open-ended survey before they come to the interview (such as the one in Figure 5-1).
2. *Try to have a one-on-one visit with every board member.* Try to go to their office or home. It is respectful to go to someone else's home or place of business. Don't ask them to come to your office. You are the "new kid" on the block.
3. *Get acquainted with city officials, especially the city manager.* Be careful not to be too pushy. If the city manager is in the direct chain of command over you, you could send a wrong signal with an invitation to lunch. A short get-acquainted visit in his or her office might be the most appropriate first move.
4. *Get acquainted with the business people in town.* Take the executive director of the Chamber of Commerce to lunch and try to discover the names of key business people you need to know. Take one or more of them to lunch every week.
5. *Visit at least two other libraries of the same size in your state.* It honors them, and you will learn more in a two-hour visit than a whole semester in a class in library school. In fact, I recommend library visits as one of the most valuable continuing education activities for anyone working in a public library.

FIGURE 5-1   Staff Get-Acquainted Form

Name_____

Address_____

_____

Telephone_____

In what department do you work?_____

What is your position title?_____

What are your major daily tasks?_____

_____

What do you like best about your job at the library?_____

_____

If you could change one thing about your job what would it be?

_____

What level of education have you attained?_____

What are your educational plans?_____

_____

What motivates you?_____

_____

The space that follows is for you to tell the new librarian anything you want to about yourself.

After you become acquainted with your colleagues in the state, take or send several staff members on visits to other libraries.

Unless you have been promoted from within, you are new to the territory and need to establish a network. If you wait six months to make these contacts, it will be too late. Your work patterns will already be established, and your network may not be one that will help you be most effective.

You will want to do a lot of listening and not much talking—especially about what you did in your former position. Most of the people you visit with won't care what you did in your last job.

Your most important job is to find out who has the power. This means determining who the formal and informal leaders are—on the staff, on the board and in the community. If you don't do this quickly, you may not be able to make the changes you want.

INTERVIEW THE STAFF

People don't care how much you know until they know how much you care. Your respect for staff opinions will do much to show them that you care. The most important thing about staff interviews is to find out what the staff expects of you. Try to interview everyone. This may be impossible, if the staff very large. While you will be working more closely with assistants and department heads, don't forget the shelvers and clerks. Some of the most candid responses might come from them—and they will always remember you for listening to them.

A survey form like the preceding one may help you get to know them better. Remember, this is not a hiring interview, and you are not violating their civil rights if you ask them about their family or hobbies.

VISIT WITH BOARD MEMBERS

Ask board members questions that will let them know that you are serious about their concerns. They may be more candid with you now than they were in the interview. Ask them what changes they would like to see and what their priorities are for the library. Here are a few questions you might try:

- What do you consider the library's most pressing need in the next six months?
- What is the most pressing need in the next year?
- If you were the new librarian, what is the first thing you would do?
- Give me the names of two or three people in the community who could help the library the most.

- What do you think members of the library board expect of the new director?
- How does the community feel about the library?

As you visit with board members, remember that they may not know very much about the day-to-day operations of the library. Their job is to represent the community in the running of the library. Ask them questions about the community. They can give you an insider's view of the people in town.

SET A PERSONAL VISION

Getting acquainted is essential to your success as the director of the library, but eventually you have roll up your sleeves and go to work. You need to do some serious planning with the staff and board, but you need to establish your personal vision for the library first. My personal vision for the libraries I am responsible for is "to give the people what they want when they come to the library." You may develop a wider vision of reaching out to those who have never found their way to the library. They may not even know that the library has information they have never though about wanting. Setting your personal vision for the library will send a clear message to the board, to the staff and to the community that you are serious about your job.

SUMMARY

Stephen Covey's sixth "Habit of Highly Effective People" is "synergize." "Synergy results from vaulting differences by bringing different perspectives together in the spirit of mutual respect. Insecure people tend to make others over in their own image and surround themselves with people who think similarly. They mistake uniformity for unity, sameness for oneness. Real oneness means complimentariness."

The relationship the board has with the librarian is the key to a smoothly run library. When librarians understand the board's concern for their performance and when trustees understand that the librarian wants what is best for the library, they will achieve unity. Eliminating barriers and keeping the channels of communication open is the key to working together.

POLICY

All policy decisions rest on an uncertain future; therefore, every policy made today is at risk tomorrow

J. P. Leemhuis

No one is more responsible for the library's policy than the board of trustees. The effective library policy is a carefully written document, refined by the test of time. It is a blueprint for library operation, an administrative guide for the librarian, a rule book for the staff, and a bill of rights for the public. To see how your library policy touches almost everything the library board does, count the number of motions at your next board meeting that relate to policies. Library hours, loan periods, staff vacations, and budget are all policy decisions. Policies are the basis for programs.

Good staff morale is critical to a well-run library. The staff will feel better about policy changes if they are involved in the process.

When formulating or reviewing library policy, begin by asking yourself: "What do we want to accomplish with this policy?" Then write your policy. When you have finished, ask yourself: "Will this policy do what we want it to do?"

What is the purpose of a policy that fines customers if they return library materials late? Some say it is to generate more revenue for the library, or to punish delinquent borrowers, or to make the books available to more people. The only good answer is to get the books back.

If your policy is designed to punish delinquent borrowers, it may only serve to discourage people from borrowing books. The negative public relations of a policy that punishes people could be devastating to the library at budget time.

Although you want your overdue policy to guarantee that every piece of material checked out from your library is returned, there is no way you can write library policy that will control the behavior of your patrons to the point that every book is returned on time, or even returned at all.

CREATING POLICY

At the basis of almost every policy is a deep-seated fear. We are afraid that someone will do something that will hurt the library, the board, the librarian, or the staff.

For several years the Great Bend Public Library had two library cards: one for adults and one for children. Adults could check out any book in the library. Children could only check out material in the children's section. Junior high school children could get an adult card. When we reviewed our policy, board members asked: *What is the purpose of this policy?* The answer was: to keep children from borrowing materials intended for adults. *What is so bad about that?* Well, some parents might object to their child having a certain book. *What can the parents do?* They could complain and ask us to remove the book from our shelves. Because we are afraid of a censorship battle, we write a policy to protect ourselves.

The Great Bend library board solved the problem with a policy statement that puts the responsibility for what children read where it truly belongs—on the parents, not on the library.

> Circulation Policy: The library, in accordance with its book selection policy, will select materials on a variety of topics representing all points of view. Library staff members will not restrict the circulation of books based on age. Parents who sign this card agree to the following: 1) They are responsible for maintaining the physical condition of the books checked out by their children including loss, damage or overdue; 2) They are wholly responsible for monitoring the appropriateness of materials their children check out.
>
> Signature parent or guardian_____

We now have only one card for both children and adults. Parents sign the card of school children living at home.

A positively worded book selection policy, based on "The Library Bill of Rights" and the "Freedom to Read Statement," is a powerful weapon against those who believe that some books should not be read by anyone. Policy assures collection development from all points of view and provides equal access to all citizens. If you are armed beforehand, the battle could be over before it starts. (See Appendix A, "Citizen Request for Reconsideration of a Book," and Appendix C, "Great Bend Public Library Book Selection Policy.")

A good library policy is stable and reasonable enough to withstand challenges from those who disagree with it, yet flexible enough to allow for exceptions when warranted. Active library boards review their policies annually to make sure the policy meets the needs of the stated objectives.

Ten years ago most libraries didn't need policies on computers, videotape collections or database searching, but today these services are standard, and the library needs a policy to regulate them. Regularly scheduled reviews will guarantee that the policy meets current situations.

Good Library Policy:

—Is fair to everyone including staff
—Is flexible enough to meet the exceptions that always occur
—Is written in simple, concise language
—Is accessible to anyone who wants a copy
—Supports the mission statement of the library
—Opens doors to service
—Is based on need to provide equal access to everyone
—Defines the library in positive terms
—Is empowering to patrons.

Questionable Library Policy:

—Is punitive, especially to specific groups
—Is challenging to read and understand
—Is difficult for library staff to interpret and enforce
—Is unnecessarily restrictive or authoritarian.

EVALUATING POLICY

Once adopted, library policy should have the support of the entire board, the librarian, and the staff. The board, the director, and the library staff should be able to explain the policy and the reasons for it at any time.

CHECKLIST FOR REVIEWING LIBRARY POLICY

1. Is this policy absolutely essential for the operation of the library, the protection of the board, the librarian, and the staff?
2. Does this policy protect the rights of all who use the library to have equal access to information?

3. Can this policy be administered fairly by the board, the librarian, or the staff?
4. Does this policy support the mission statement of the library?
5. Is this policy worded so that it cannot be misunderstood or interpreted ?
6. Does this policy treat protected groups fairly? (People grouped by race, religion, sex, age, national origin, or disability)
7. Is there a hidden agenda or ulterior motive connected with this policy?
8. Is this policy positively stated rather than filled with prohibitions against certain behaviors?

Unless you are organizing a new library, you probably have a written policy somewhere. It may not be up-to-date, but you have one. When was the last time you reviewed it?

Some time in the next six months, why not sit down with your librarian and other members of your board to review and revise your library's policy? Unless the board is used to working as a committee-of-the-whole, the board chair needs to appoint a committee of two or three people to work with the librarian.

Start by finding the most recent copy of your policy. When was it last revised? Chances are that you have made a few changes in specific policies at regular board meetings during the past year. Review the minutes of all board meetings since the date of the last policy revision. Make copies of any policy changes made at board meetings and distribute them to committee members. Check with the state library to learn of any changes in the law that might have an impact on your library. Give committee members an opportunity to review the material, then call them together.

START WITH A MISSION STATEMENT

Start by reviewing the library's mission statement. This will help you focus on the goals of the library and give you the opportunity to propose changes. If you don't have a mission statement, write one. It may require more than one session, and the librarian should involve the staff in the process. This could delay the policy review process, but it is worth it. The important thing about a mission statement is its power to focus the board, the staff, and the public on the purposes of the library. When the library's mission statement is clear to everyone, policies will be easier to set and understand, budgets will be easier to create, and programs will occur naturally to meet the needs of the patrons.

Your mission statement defines your organization for your patrons (clients or customers). It helps the staff focus their energies and set priorities. A good mission statement lets people know what they can expect when they come to you for service. It should be short enough for the staff to memorize, clear enough to be understood by anyone, and clever enough to capture the imagination of everyone.

Brainstorming can produce exciting, often unexpected, results. You sit down with a group of people who have the library's interest in common and can think creatively. Set aside one half hour of uninterrupted time. Assign one person to be note taker. Some brainstorming facilitators I know like to use newsprint sheets on an easel or big sheets, taped to the wall. Select a leader whose job it is to direct the discussion. The facilitator encourages participation by making positive statements about the process. For example: "We are going great. Let's keep it up. What else can we think of?" The leader reminds everyone of the rules, if that becomes necessary.

RULES FOR BRAINSTORMING

1. *Appoint a time keeper and set a time limit.* Twenty minutes is usually an optimum amount for the creative phase of brainstorming
2. *Everyone contributes.* You can start by going around the table. If a person can't think of anything the first time around, move on to the next person. Maybe he or she will the next time. Soon everyone will respond spontaneously.
3. *Write down all ideas as they are given.* The leader may repeat what has been said to give the contributor a chance to clarify the idea.
4. *Make no evaluation of any kind at this time.* Negative comments are especially discouraged, as are negative body language or laughing at an idea.

Brainstorming works best when the group focuses on a specific question: What is the mission of our library? Write your focus question on a chalkboard or separate chart where participants can see it as they brainstorm.

Once people loosen up and get into the process, ideas will flow like water. I heard of a group of seven secretaries who came up with 256 ideas in one 20-minute brainstorming session. It took five of them to write down all of the ideas. They weren't hampered by restraining thoughts of what wouldn't work or negative consequences of expressing their ideas. Of course, not all of the ideas were used. But some outlandish ideas become the springboard for many good ones.

DEVELOPING A MISSION STATEMENT

- Sit down with your staff and/or your board and brainstorm.
- Allow 20 minutes for the process.
- Write responses on a flip chart or chalkboard.
- Go around the group in order and complete this sentence: (Name your organization) is in business to . . . .
- Or you can use one-word descriptions. The one word that describes what (your organizations name) does is . . . .
- Once you have a list of statements about your organization, combine similar statements and analyze them.
- Circle key words and rank them by priority. What two or three words best describe the most important functions of your organization?
- Begin writing your mission statement by saying: We at (name of your organization) are in the _____ business. Libraries are in the information business, not the book business. Hospitals are in the wellness business, not caring for the sick.
- Next say, "Our mission is to . . . ."
- You can expand your mission statement (though it is not necessary) by saying, "We accomplish our mission by . . . ." Using numbers or bullets (•) you can list some of the services of the organization, but be sure to do it in terms of benefits to the users.
- Once you have a rough draft of your mission statement, write it down and let it cool for a week or more. Discuss it at your next meeting. Give everyone the opportunity to change it, revise it, or scrap it altogether and start over.

Keep your mission statement as brief as possible. The more words you use, the more difficult it will be to memorize and the less chance it will have of being internalized by the staff and the board.

Once you are satisfied with the statement you have developed, publish it for the world to see—especially the staff and the board. Put it on your letterhead, if it is short enough. Include it in your advertising. Put it on a plaque, which you hang behind the front desk. If you just write it in your policy manual, no one will see it and your mission statement will be soon forgotten.

After a year, ask yourself, "Has our mission changed? Has our business focus changed?" If things have changed, revise your mission statement. Remember it is designed to define your organization for your clients (customers) and help the staff focus their energies on organizational priorities. It doesn't have to be cast in stone forever.

A POLICY REVIEW IN TENNESSEE

With your mission statement in place, it is time to review or write your policy. It could be a very positive experience for you. It was for Clara Hasbrouck, a board member of the Sullivan County Public Library in Kingsport, Tennessee.

Here is what they did:

1. The director and committee of boards collected board minutes and directives concerning:
   • Operation of main library and branches;
   • Personnel policy; and
   • Circulation and selection of materials.
2. Through a series of meetings they:
   • Reviewed procedures and practices;
   • Discussed how policies worked and problems; and
   • Researched compatibility with other applicable county documents.
3. They wrote the manual and presented it to the board for review and approval and the staff for information and use.
4. They reviewed and revised it annually as needed.

They considered the project a success because they ended up with a single document with answers to some problems. They found the process to be valuable, too: Trustees and the director were willing to discuss (even disagree) and arrive at a workable solution.

They caution to others who might become involved in creating a policy manual to:

1. Involve more of the staff from the very beginning.
2. Be specific in designating what are policies (board responsibility) what are operational procedures (director responsibility or a function management).
3. Thoroughly research what documents you have. Differentiate between what is 'tradition' and what is policy. (Be very careful of the former!)
4. Alleviate fears about any changes by labeling the first document a "working draft" so the staff understands it is not the final word.

5. Do a "pilot" of any big changes—try them first and evaluate results before making them final. It is worth the extra time.

POLICIES VERSUS PROCEDURES

Sometimes when writing policy we tend to mix in procedure . In fact, some libraries have a policy and procedures manual. Procedure is the responsibility of the library director, not the library board. The board sets policy and the librarian carries it out. As you write each policy, ask yourself, "How much of this policy is procedure?" Some spelling out of procedure may be necessary to insure that the policy is administered properly, but please let the librarian run the library.

Are you ready now to tackle the task of revising your policies? My final how-to-do-it help for writing library policy is in Appendix B, which presents an outline for library policy with guidelines (reasons for having the policy), a sample policy, and space to write your own policy. It might be handier to photocopy the pages and put them in a looseleaf notebook. However you use them, they are designed to give you ideas as you work through the process of developing the policies for your own library.

No matter how hard you try, you can't cover everything with a policy. The list for possible policies is inexhaustible. You could have a policy on dogs in the library or latch-key children, or any topic you may have a problem with. Here are a few things we did not include in Appendix B that you may wish to consider:

- Disposition of gifts the library cannot use
- Unattended children below a certain age
- Fees for certain services
- Food or drink in the library
- Serving of alcoholic beverages in the library
- Standards for behavior of patrons using the library
- Use of audiovisual equipment
- Procedure to implement federal copyright law
- Book deposit for return of library books
- Property risk management
- Special loan policies for special materials (i.e., videos, compact discs.)
- Cooperation with regional library systems
- Reserves for school classes
- Holds for patrons

If you need other sample policies, borrow a copy of *Public Library Policy Resource Manual* (Michigan Library Assn., 415 Kalamazoo, Lansing, MI 48933), which represents a broad range of sample policies.

SUMMARY

Creating policy requires that the board and the library director work together. Each brings a perspective essential to the final product. The librarian has to implement the policy and knows what will work and what won't. The board can be a little more philosophical. Trustees can say what "ought" to be without making it happen. They bring the patron perspective to the table. They can even ask, "Why do we need this rule?" Take a fresh look at your policies. Remember, you are empowering people to use your library to better themselves, enjoy life more, become better informed, and enhance their talents. Don't create policies that make it difficult for them.

7 SECURING AND MANAGING MONEY

All economic progress is based on the innate desire of every organism to live beyond it means.

Murphy

State law usually guarantees an income for all legally established public libraries, but it is the job of the library board to see that the library income is adequate and well-managed. Budgeting is the process of allocating current resources and securing additional funds, if needed. The library's budget is its single most important planning document. It sets the board's priorities for the expenditure of funds. It should be written down and referred to regularly as part of the monthly financial statement.

The librarian is the one who best knows the day-to-day operation and expenses of the library. The librarian knows when the building needs maintenance, what books people will want to read, and what supplies to buy. Once fixed costs are allocated, it is the board's responsibility to establish priorities for programs and services. Setting salary increases based on the librarian's recommendations is also the board's responsibility. Operational expenditures are the responsibility of the librarian. Budget functions that relate to policy belong to the board. So together, the board and the librarian work on the budget, and in the end, the board adopts it.

BUDGETING

You can divide budgeting into four steps:

1. Determine all available resources, including tax funds, state aid, grants and gifts, fines, memorials, and endowment funds.
2. Identify all potential expenditures over which the board has little control (e.g., utilities, employee benefits, rent, and base line salaries). Allocate funds for these.
3. Allocate funds for expenditures over which the board has *almost* no control (e.g., postage, building maintenance, supplies).
4. Finally, allocate the remaining funds among those expenditures over which the library has absolute control (e.g., salary increases, books, travel).

93

I like to wait until we have the expenditure totals from the previous year before finalizing budget allocations. Last year's expenditures for fixed costs are helpful in projecting realistic figures for next year. Once the fixed costs are set, other priorities can follow.

LIBRARY BUDGET CHECKLIST

General

- Is our budget written down?
- Does every board member and the librarian have a copy?
- Does everyone understand the budget?

Revenue

- Does our budget include all anticipated revenue including direct cash payments made by other agencies for items such as utilities, maintenance, and insurance?
- Do we know the expenditure restrictions on various revenue sources?
- If our library needs more money, what can we do to increase our income?

Expenditures

- Have we realistically allocated all of our resources?
- Is there enough money budgeted in each category to do the programs we want to do?
- Do we have a contingency plan for unexpected expenditures?
- Does our budget incorporate the thinking of the librarian and of a majority of the board?
- Does everyone feel *good* about the budget?

WORKING WITH STAFF TO PLAN THE BUDGET

One respondent who requested to remain anonymous shared a new process for involving staff in the budgeting process.

Our staff was frustrated over limited budgets year after year. They saw no positive action on their requests to the director. In the past, the staff heads made requests to the director, who alone decided which ones to support. The director made up budget and presented it, *fait accompli*, to the board, who supported it at city budget committee.

FIGURE 7-1   Sample Budgeting Form

Revenue	Actual 1992	Budgeted 1993	Proposed 1994
City mill levy, etc.	_____	_____	_____
System grant	_____	_____	_____
State aid	_____	_____	_____
Other sources revenue	_____	_____	_____
Total Revenue	_____	_____	_____

Expenditures	Actual 1992	Budgeted 1993	Proposed 1994
Salaries	_____	_____	_____
Salaries paid by others	_____	_____	_____
Benefits	_____	_____	_____
Total Personnel	_____	_____	_____
Books	_____	_____	_____
Magazines	_____	_____	_____
Other materials	_____	_____	_____
Total Materials	_____	_____	_____
Electricity	_____	_____	_____
Natural Gas	_____	_____	_____
Maintenance	_____	_____	_____
Postage	_____	_____	_____
Supplies	_____	_____	_____
Travel	_____	_____	_____
Other	_____	_____	_____
Total Operations	_____	_____	_____
Overall Total	_____	_____	_____

Staff involvement in the creation of the budget and the spending of the money is critical to morale. The library director needs to involve staff in the process as much as possible and then give them authority and control over a segment of the budget. With that authority goes their accountability to the director.

A new process, initiated at board request, was to have staff department heads present all budgetary requests to a group that included the director, the board, and other staff department heads. In follow-up sessions, the board and director prioritized requests (staff invited to attend). From that list, the director made up budget, and the board sold it to the city.

As a result, staff morale increased—even if their requests were turned down, they saw why and how. They also saw success overall. The board was now fully informed and could really sell it to the city, point by point, from a position of deep conviction and understanding. Some items were best allocated to other support: requests to Friends, local business, etc. Thus resources were brought to bear. The director was no longer in cross-fire and has a more satisfied staff.

GETTING MORE TAX REVENUE

Contributions and gifts can be solicited, but long-term solutions will probably require a tax fund increase. Learn the legal procedures for doing this and go for it. If your library is a viable, appreciated organization in the community, you have a good chance. Remember, however: performance precedes funding. Requesting from a position of strength is better than begging from a position of weakness. (See also *Fundraising for the Small Public Library,* which has a chapter on increasing tax dollars for the library.)

GETTING THE BUDGET ADOPTED

The adopted budget should be forwarded to the governing body, within the time frame they have established and by whatever communication channels have been established. Most cities hold their budget hearings about six months before the beginning of the next fiscal year.

Some libraries have a fixed millage set aside for library purposes; others must plead for an appropriation every year. If your library is one of the latter, the outline in Figure 7-1 may help you. It may help those who have the opportunity to increase their funds at budget time.

Establish the library as a viable, valuable service.

- People use your library—e.g., "We have 4,499 registered borrowers, or 49 percent of our population. Last year they borrowed 61,467 books. That is 13.66 per borrower." Use testimonials of prominent people who use the library.
- No other agency in the city does what the library does.
- It serves the information needs of adults including the growing populations of the elderly, students, and preschool children.
- It networks with other libraries for resources it does not own.
- Special services include: delivery to the home-bound; AV equipment; a photocopier and genealogical microfilm. (Make your own list.)
- The library is doing a good job. (Brag a little.)
- The library saves people money and is cost effective. For every dollar it receives, the library returns to the public $10 in service. (Multiply your circulation times the average cost of a book.)

Use existing conditions to illustrate library's needs.

- Analyze the budget and determine the library's priorities.
- Use only the data which will point out the library's needs.
- Be specific, yet brief in describing the situation.
- Know exactly what you want and make a specific request.
- Ask for a specific amount for a specified need:
  —We need an extra $2,000 for books.
  —We want $1,500 to bring the librarian's salary up to minimum wage.
  —We need $1,700 to fix the roof of the library.

Present logical arguments that support your request.

Example: The roof of the library leaks every time it rains. The water comes in and ruins the floor and books. The library has no money to fix the roof.

Suggest ways the governing body can grant your request.

- Suggest that the city could fix the roof from the city's building maintenance fund.

- Request other state and federal funds the city may have at its disposal.

INCREASING THE LIBRARY BUDGET

Tax-supported institutions find it difficult to continue current programs when revenue levels remain constant over a period of years. Libraries in particular are finding their share of the pie getting smaller. Why resign ourselves to fate when we can keep on fighting? Here are some ideas that have worked in other areas.

1. Encourage patrons to *adopt a magazine* for a year by paying for the subscription. When magazines are being cut from a subscription list, some people may want to rescue their favorite magazine. Try a bulletin board with a stork or a baby bassinet framing each magazine title with its price. Ask your patrons to become adoptive "magazine parents."

2. *Ask for JPTA or Green Thumb personnel.* These federally funded programs provide jobs to youth and other members of low-income families. They need good work sites like the library. Contact your local Job Service office. Treat these workers just like other employees. If they don't work out, don't be afraid to let them go. Be sure to document their activities before you take action.

3. *Organize a Friends of the Library group.* They can conduct fundraising activities on behalf of the library. Although fundraising can provide a lot of money for the library, it can also be time-consuming for the library staff. Better to offer help getting a Friends group started than to try to do it yourself. Fundraising for a big-ticket item can be more successful than raising money for more books or salaries. People like to see a major result of their effort and generosity. If you need help getting organized, contact Friends of Libraries U.S.A., American Library Association, 50 E. Huron, Chicago, IL 60611. They are a national organization that works to develop and support local and state Friends groups throughout the country.

4. Make sure your library is getting its *fair share* of available tax funds. Even though the city budget is growing each year, the library's share may be getting smaller and smaller. Check it out. Gather your data and make a case for your library.

5. Request that the city pay for some of the following from other budgets:

- *Social Security and retirement payments.* This can save the library 13 percent or more of its personnel budget. Some cities have an employee benefit fund.

- *Utilities*. If the city owns the library, it may be willing to pay for utilities.
- *Insurance on the building*. The library could be covered with a blanket policy with other city buildings.
- *Custodial service*. This can save your library two or three percent.
- *Lawn and grounds upkeep*. The park crews may be able to take care of the library's lawn at no additional cost to the city.

CREATING A FOUNDATION

A library foundation is a legally established nonprofit organization formed for the specific purpose of receiving charitable gifts for the library. It is organized to become qualified as a 501(c)(3) tax-exempt entity. If a fundraising effort by the library is offset by a reduction in tax support, a foundation or a Friends group is a *must*. These are the only ways to protect donations that might come to the library, short of obtaining an agreement from the governing body to let you keep the money you raise without reducing taxes.

Foundation Success in Minneapolis

Jack Cole, a trustee from Minnesota's Hennepin County Library, tells of his success in organizing the library foundation.

> While president of the board (1984-88), the librarian, Robert Rohlf and I agreed on the need for a separate foundation board to receive funds for our collection, staff development, and immigrant literacy program that could not be funded with public dollars.

> We decided to create a separate foundation board of men and women of influence who support the Hennepin County Library, but who were never asked to help and engage them and others in an issue (immigrant literacy) that was timely.

> The Hennepin County Library Foundation was incorporated in 1986 with the approval of the Hennepin County Commissioners by the Library Board, who recognized that a great library system must remain flexible and responsive to provide the services only a library can to the people of suburban Hennepin County.

> Very simply, the Foundation is a nonprofit organization

whose purpose is to provide books and services not otherwise available to the Hennepin County Library System.

We were able to recruit our board, define our mission, plan creatively, and raise $279,000 in 14 months for the foundation and its projects. If we could do it over again, we would spend more time qualifying foundation members and recruiting more power people.

Jack's advice to others seeking to organize a foundation is: "Take the risk and ask for help once you have worked on the need. Do not be afraid to approach moneyed individuals." (Also see *Fundraising for the Small Public Library*, which has a chapter on organizing a Friends group and creating a library foundation and includes sample by-laws and purpose statements.)

PRINCIPLES OF FUNDRAISING

While asking (selling) may be the most important step to fundraising, it is not quite that simple. If it were, we wouldn't need books on the subject. Fundraisers have developed some techniques that help us organize our efforts and refine our methods so that we can raise more money with less effort and be successful more of the time.

Let's start with five principles of fundraising. They are essential to any successful fundraising effort.

1. *Know how much you need and the purpose of your project:* If you don't know the total cost of your project or why you need the money, your commitment will be weak. You don't have to share your goal with the donor, but you need to have it clearly in mind.

2. *Give before you ask:* Everyone who asks others for money must give to their cause themselves. They must give enough to make a difference in the cause or in their own lives.

3. *Ask for the gift:* If you don't ask, you won't get. (At least most of the time.) Some libraries have been known to receive large gifts from unknown or unexpected sources. Don't count on it!

4. *Ask the right person for the right amount:* You don't pick one-pound tomatoes from a cherry tomato plant. You have to do your research if you want to know who to ask for a big gift.

5. *Say thank you:* Say thank you as many ways as you can. And

recognize everyone who helped. Someone has said that you have to say thank you seven times before you can ask for another gift.

REDUCING EXPENDITURES

If all efforts to increase revenue fall short, the only alternative is to reduce expenditures. It is wise to reduce costs that do not affect service. Most libraries have been doing that for so long that there is nothing left to give. Salary increases and books are the most vulnerable to budget cuts, yet these two items can affect service most.

REDUCING THE LIBRARY BUDGET

The key to reducing library expenditures is to do so without reducing services. Remember that performance precedes funding. A reduction in service is the least desirable of all alternatives because it reduces your perceived performance. You can shift the financial responsibility for some functions without reducing service. Here are some ideas worth investigating.

Take full advantage of system services: If your system provides a service at cost, are you duplicating that service or function in your library? Not all libraries take full advantage of the system processing services, but it could save them thousands of hours if they would.

Use more interlibrary loans: Small libraries cannot afford to buy every new bestseller. If you project that a certain book will only circulate once or twice in your area, wouldn't it be smart to secure it on interlibrary loan? A book circulated only once is a very expensive circulation. Buy books you know will circulate several times.

Double staff only in peak periods: Unless you are having story hour or circulate more than 50-75 books per hour, you probably don't need more than one person on circulation duty at a time.

Establish hours that serve the people best: Nothing is more inefficient than to have the library open when the people don't use it. As much as possible, the library should be open during the same hours every day, so people can get used to the hours. Even in the smallest of towns, evening and weekend hours are appreciated.

Reduce energy costs: Make building and equipment improvements that will save energy. A $1,500 investment in night setback (air handling) equipment saved the Great Bend Public Library $1,700 in electricity cost the first nine months it was installed. Storm windows and caulking around windows and doors can save fuel costs.

Use volunteers: They can be trained to do many important tasks and thus feel important to the library. Don't use them for the menial tasks, like dusting shelves or shelving books unless they really enjoy that kind of work. The Great Bend Public Library has a volunteer who really loves to replace worn out book jackets and another volunteer who enjoys filing catalog cards.

Simplify the work: Review all tasks. Eliminate the ones that don't need doing. Too often a task is done because "that's the way it has always been done." Time spent doing clerical tasks can often be eliminated in favor of serving the public.

CUTTING TO THE BONE

Many libraries around the country are finding it necessary to make severe cuts in their budgets—closing branches, laying off staff, reducing hours. When they come, the stress on everyone—from the president of the board to the library director to the book shelver—is unbelievable. Here are a few tips I have learned from personal experience:

- Involve as many people as possible in the planning for the reductions.
- Try to develop some consensus about where the cuts should come from.
- Look for solutions that will not affect staff first.
- Look for solutions that will have a negative impact on the least number of patrons.
- Cut discretionary spending first.
- If you have to lay off staff, do it where the loss will least affect public services.

- If you have to lay off staff, do it once and for all (cutting deep enough the first time). Then reassure the remaining staff that their jobs are secure. Tell them again and again.

BUDGETING TIME LINE

Deadlines have a way of surprising us. This guideline for preparing the budget outlines suggested deadlines for the preparation of your budget using the calendar year as the fiscal year. Local situations may vary, so change this one to meet your needs.

December or early January: Adopt the final draft of the budget for the coming year. If you wait until after all the expenses for the past year are in, information on actual expenditures will help you forecast next year's expenditure. It is all right to do it earlier, but you won't have as much inform·tion to work with then.

February city council meeting: If you intend to ask for a mill levy increase for next year, present the request to the governing body early in the fiscal year. This provides them with the opportunity to put it on the ballot for the April election if they want to let the people vote on it.

April: Draft the preliminary budget and discuss it in the April or May board meeting. You will have time to change it before you present it to the city council.

May board meeting: Adopt the final version of proposed budget. This is the budget you will give to the city for inclusion in its budget. The final amount of your budget will not be established.

June: Present the proposed budget to the city by the date requested.

September: Review the budget prior to final adoption.

November: Establish salaries. By now the income is fixed and you should be able to determine salaries for the coming year.

Budget preparation is a year-long activity. It is the single most important planning document you have. Give it your best attention.

FINANCIAL STATEMENT

Once the budget is adopted, it's time to create the format for the financial statement. The financial statement accurately reflects the fiscal condition of the library at the end of the reporting period. By carefully analyzing it, you can detect avoidable problems. By working together, the board and the librarian can plan expenditures for the year.

A good financial statement will do the following:

- Accurately represent the library's financial condition.
- Give a detailed listing of paid invoices for the month, including each vendor's name, the purpose of the expenditure, and the amount paid.
- List budget line items and detail monthly and year-to-date expenditures, with remaining balances for every budget item and the percentage spent year-to-date.
- Give an accounting of revenue received by fund, with year-to-date income received and balances remaining to be received.
- List total paid invoices, reconciled to the budget, and display the total monthly expenditures.
- Report on cash on hand.

The financial statement should be prepared by the person who keeps the library's financial records—the treasurer, the librarian, or a bookkeeper or an accounting firm paid by the board. If possible the report should be prepared, copied, and distributed before the board meeting.

FIDUCIARY RESPONSIBILITIES

The law imposes high standards of fiduciary responsibilities upon library boards. Managing funds is one of the highest legal obligations of a board, particularly when the funds are from taxes. Board members' legal responsibilities are divided into three areas:

- The duty of care to avoid mismanagement
- The duty of care to avoid non-management, and
- The duty of loyalty.

The duty of care not to mismanage rests upon traditional common law standards, which is the care exercised by a reasonable person in the management of his own affairs of like magnitude and importance. This encompasses more than just accepting the professional staff's reports. A board member must question, probe, and analyze.

LIABILITY INSURANCE

The only practical way a trustee may be accorded personal protection from liability is through insurance. It is important that the insurance policy clearly extend coverage to the members of the board. There is no easily ascertainable standard or accepted amount for this insurance coverage. The board member should look at the potential for damages in cooperation with the library's attorney to determine the insurance limits.

Some cities have liability policies that can be extended to library board members. No insurance is available to protect library board members from legal action and the award of damages from unjustified dismissal.

Commensurate with the affirmative duty of care not to mismanage is the negative duty of care labeled—*the duty to avoid non-management*. Non-management is the failure to manage at all. A board member should not rely upon another's representations, or have a superficial knowledge of the organization's activities. It is important to know the contents of the statutory authority, the by-laws, internal rules, regulations, and procedures, and the minutes of meetings. A board member should study these documents and know their contents. (The above discussion on the legal implications of board service was used with permission from: *Legal and Practical Aspects of Boardsmanship* by Eugene T. Hackler, P.O. Box 1, Olathe, Kansas 66061, no date.)

SUMMARY

Securing adequate funds for the library is clearly a board responsibility. Trustees can rely on the help of the librarian, but trustee effort cannot be seen as self-serving (e.g., to get a raise). Managing the library's budget is primarily the librarian's job, with some oversight and fiduciary responsibilities being accorded to the board. Though board members often have to rely on the expertise of their librarian, they are still accountable for the financial condition of the library.

PROVIDING ADEQUATE FACILITIES

No place affords a more striking conviction of the vanity of human hopes than a public library.

Samuel Johnson

BUILDING DO'S AND DON'TS

- Do plan for adequate space for the next 20 years.
- Don't buy an old building (to fix up) with a flat roof. It is sure to leak.
- Do plan to spend more than your architect says.
- Do start with a plan based on current and projected services.
- Don't buy an existing building (to remodel) that isn't as sound as a new building.
- Do try for a new building. Remodeling an *old* building could cost you more per square foot than tearing down and starting from scratch.

The need for a new, updated, or remodeled library building seems to be the target of most library fundraising efforts. Most libraries "make do" with the revenue they receive from taxes and a few unsolicited gifts. A library board can muddle through for years wishing they had a new library, and then one day a new board member will come on the board and inspire the others to take action.

Even though you may know that you need a new library, you may not have a precise understanding of what your needs are. Figure 8-1 is a worksheet that will help you assess your building needs.

Madalyn Davis, a trustee for the Jim Checotah Public Library, reports her success in getting a new library for Hichita, Oklahoma:

> The library is housed in a small storefront building on the main street of a rural town of 3,500 people. It is a branch of the Eastern Oklahoma District Library System, a six-county multi-library system.
>
> It immediately became apparent that the library was "bulging at the seams." We had to have more space, but there was no place to enlarge.
>
> Our five-member board and the librarian contacted the executive director of the system for help. Her enthusiasm matched ours, and with her professional advice the board and librarian called a meeting for concerned citizens who wanted a new library.
>
> A varied representation of 26 citizens joined together. Committees were formed to visit libraries throughout the state. Two local citizens (brothers) donated the site for a new library. An architect was hired to draw up the plans. Half of the funds were obtained through grants and donations. The other half came from a one-cent city sales tax (a portion of which was earmarked for the new library). The library board, citizen committees, and Friends of the Library mounted an organized telephone campaign, and the one-cent sales tax passed three to one.

It has taken almost three years, but in October 1991 a new, 6,400 square-foot library will be completed on a beautiful lot with 30 parking spaces. This was accomplished through the concerted effort of a five-member library board and the librarian, citizen's committees, and Friends of the Library, with the cooperation of the Checotah City Council and the entire community.

Madalyn Davis says their key to success was "the patience and perseverance of the library board of trustees, the librarian, and the citizen committees. It proves that a small group of people can get an entire community involved." Her advice to others is, "Know what you want, get an organized plan, and stay with it."

WORKING INDEPENDENTLY

My friend Maurice P. Marchant tells of a project that had a less than positive outcome. Perhaps it will be valuable as an example of what can happen when groups in support of a project work independently.

The library board worked in one direction; the Friends group worked in another; and in the end the mayor took charge of things, leaving many people with hurt feelings. The project was the construction of a new public library building that would be adequate for a city of 80,000. But the final product was a library that was grossly inadequate even before it was dedicated. This is Maurice Marchant's account:

> An attempt at public approval of a bond issue had been defeated narrowly several years earlier. The Friends viewed the projected new building as necessary for improving library service. For us, it was a means, not the end. And we were concerned that operation funds be increased to provide the resources required to give adequate service.
>
> In 1983, the president of the Friends started a PR campaign to alert the citizens of the library's inadequacies and the reasons for improving them. She was sufficiently successful that the library board decided the time was right to renew their building project. The city librarian was supportive and worked in concert with the board. The board encouraged the mayor

FIGURE 8-1 Building Needs Analysis Worksheet

	Yes	No	Comments
Plant Exterior			
Inviting/appealing	___	___	_____
Meets fire codes	___	___	_____
Roof in good condition	___	___	_____
Energy Efficiency			
Ceiling insulated	___	___	_____
Walls insulated	___	___	_____
Windows efficient	___	___	_____
Doors efficient	___	___	_____
Foundation			
Structurally sound	___	___	_____
Moisture proof	___	___	_____
Proper drainage	___	___	_____
Entrances/Exits			
Easy to open/close	___	___	_____
All weather (covered)	___	___	_____
Easily accessed (stairs)	___	___	_____
Handicapped accessed	___	___	_____
Location			
High traffic area	___	___	_____
Available to mass transit	___	___	_____
Adequate parking	___	___	_____
Handicapped parking	___	___	_____
Well lit at night	___	___	_____
Visibility			
Effective signing	___	___	_____
Hours visible from street	___	___	_____
"LIBRARY" in 4+ inch letters	___	___	_____

FIGURE 8-1 *Cont'd.*

Plant Interior

Heating and Cooling	Yes	No	Comments
Good condition	—	—	_____
Energy efficient	—	—	_____
Humidity control	—	—	_____

Flooring, Walls, and Ceiling

Good condition	—	—	_____
Acoustical	—	—	_____
Pleasant appearance	—	—	_____

Basic Layout

Aids traffic flow	—	—	_____
Handicapped access	—	—	_____
All areas controllable	—	—	_____
Elevator for multi-levels	—	—	_____
Rest rooms	—	—	_____
Child access	—	—	_____

Electrical and Lighting

Under 10 years old	—	—	_____
AV and cable support	—	—	_____
Computer support	—	—	_____
Phone and modem support	—	—	_____
Adequate outlets	—	—	_____
Suitable lighting all areas	—	—	_____
100 ft. candle in study areas	—	—	_____

FIGURE 8-1 *Cont'd.*

Adequacy of space

Public Areas	Yes	No	Comments
Circulation area	___	___	_____
Reference area	___	___	_____
Public catalog area	___	___	_____
Display areas	___	___	_____
Information areas	___	___	_____
AV use areas	___	___	_____
Computer area	___	___	_____
Book stack areas	___	___	_____
Reading areas	___	___	_____
Children's area	___	___	_____
Storytelling area	___	___	_____
Young adult area	___	___	_____
Small conference rooms	___	___	_____
Multi-use auditorium	___	___	_____
Refreshment area	___	___	_____

Staff Areas			
Office space	___	___	_____
Work space	___	___	_____
Conference space	___	___	_____
Storage area	___	___	_____
Staff break area	___	___	_____
Book sorting area	___	___	_____

(Source: Vance Associates, LeMars, Iowa)

and the municipal council to move forward on the project, giving them funds to hire an architect to design preliminary plans for a new structure.

Since the mayor and council wanted to keep city taxes as low as possible, the board was told to set up a fundraising project. Board members sent out letters and assigned volunteers to contact people in different occupational categories. The board also ran a telethon. A local bank loaned its telephone resources to the board during evening hours over a two-week period. Those who agreed to donate were sent thank-you's and donation forms, and the city set up an automated file to control information regarding donations.

The Friends carried out a variety of projects, some of them fundraisers such as book sales, read-a-thons, chocolate-tasting extravaganzas, and membership drives. But the money did not go for construction. Rather, we used it to improve current services, to purchase resources that could be used in the new building, and for public relations. As no tax funds could be used in support of an impending bond election, we became the primary resource for that purpose. The Friends membership increased from about 50 to 550, and they raised about $30,000.

LSCA construction funding amounted to a little over $200,000. Along with the fundraising effort, the total was enough to qualify the library project for a large grant from a private foundation.

The next step was critical. With those resources, the board went back to the mayor to negotiate for a bond election to pay for whatever else was needed. They asked for a $2,000,000 bond to pay for the 33,000-square-foot building their architect had designed. He had given a rough estimate of $2,500,000. The mayor opposed paying any more to the architect to nail down the cost and approved a bond proposal of only $1,500,000. The municipal council went along and set the bond as an issue on the ballot at the next municipal election.

The library board set up a citizen's committee to get out the vote. We solicited help from one of the university's communications classes, which designed ads and door knockers, wrote news releases, and so forth. Many people wrote letters to the editors of local newspapers, and we wrote news stories and did radio spots on why the new building would be construct-ed. The Friends funded the costs. While the city could not take sides, it designed a flyer setting out the facts and sent copies to every home.

When the vote came in, the library bond was approved three to one. But while everyone was excited, major problems were yet to come:

1. Original architectural projections were grossly under-estimated.
2. Over 5,000 square feet had to be cut from the building, reducing it to 27,000 square feet. (At least 50,000 and up to 80,000 square feet would have been more appropriate for a city this size.)
3. The mayor took over planning for the building from the board.
4. The mayor decided to rotate the building so that its large windows faced the southeast, causing lighting and heating problems.
5. The entrance for people in wheelchairs is up a convoluted ramp that hardly anyone is willing to try.

The end result was a largely inadequate building, poorly designed, too small for present needs, and with no easy way for expansion.

The mayor not only resisted increasing the library's operating budget, but actually reduced it to provide more money for cleaning and building maintenance. The library director re-signed, as did many of his staff, as morale nose-dived. The mayor reduced hours of service by nearly 20 percent, but had to reinstate about half of those hours. Patrons also com-plained about inadequate service and the shortage of books in the new building, and the difficulties handicapped patrons experience trying to enter the building.

Failure occurred especially from the ignorance of the board and the director regarding the planning process and their failure to get accurate estimates. There was also too much closed-door decision making between the board and the mayor. Some critical decisions were kept from the public and from the Friends who were thus unable to bring political influence to bear when it might have been helpful.

The Friends have become discouraged and are no longer very

active. New board members are working to improve relations with the mayor and get his support in rectifying the problems. To the extent that the project was successful, it can be attributed to the harmony that existed among the various groups involved.

IDAHO LIBRARY DOUBLES IN SIZE

Contrast the previous summary with a "working together" experience that turned out well. Dennis S. Voorhees, a trustee of Idaho's Twin Falls Public Library, tells of the success of a project where the size of a 20,000 square-foot library was doubled using a state-administered federal grant, a successful bond election, and a successful fund drive for private donations. The total cost of the project was more than $2,000,000. Dennis Voorhees's account follows:

The key to success was an easy and trusting relationship between the library administration and library board. The trustees listened carefully to and worked closely with the library director and staff. We have an extraordinarily competent director who can both see the big picture and pay careful attention to detail.

We started with a very small circle of people and built outwards. We carefully selected consultants and worked vigorously to involve the community for review and comment. Little by little, our small circle got larger and larger. All the while there developed a sense throughout the community that the library board and administration were vitally interested in finding the right solution.

The elements contributing to the success of the undertaking were:

1. Allowing a sufficient period of time to study the issues;
2. Timely selection of feasibility and space planning consultants, building program specialists, and design architects;
3. Trustee and administration immersion in a library policy and role-setting process informing all about the needs and possibilities of the library;
4. Early and continuous consultation with the lead governmental unit—the Twin Falls City Council;
5. Early formation of a citizens' advisory group that worked

diligently in reviewing and advising the library board and city council on public needs and perceptions;

6. Careful documentation of each step: feasibility study, planning and role setting, space needs and siting requirements, citizens' advisory group study and report, building program statement, and bond initiative literature;

7. Careful understanding and development of local mythology and symbology as they relate to the library and its users;

8. Ethical process and presentation;

9. Healthy, respectful relationships with local media;

10. Careful selection and use of experts: library director, state library development specialist, library planners, architects, financial advisors, and legal advisors;

11. Thorough understanding and development of a bond referendum campaign that appreciates citizen desire for library amenities and their dislike of taxation;

12. Effective development and use of committees and written plans;

13. Thoughtful development of community vision and careful framing of challenges as opportunities;

14. Careful and comprehensive campaign planning; and

15. Effective solicitation of private individuals for capital fund and equipment and furnishing contributions (over $140,000).

The single most important element in our effort was honesty. We needed to be honest with one another, with our city council, our citizens' advisory group, the media, and the public at large. There is always the tendency by public boards to want to hold back information—especially what might be perceived as bad news. However, our experience is that the general public cannot trust a board operating in secret. I would encourage every public board to appreciate that they are instruments of public policy and not ends in themselves.

I would advise those wanting to try a similar project to take advantage of the abundance of experts and materials available to structure a successful project.

OLD TRAIN DEPOT BECOMES A LIBRARY

Susan Willis, library director in Chanute, Kansas, tells of the success her town had with raising money for a new library:

The Chanute Public Library currently occupies a Carnegie

building which has become totally inadequate for current needs. It was determined by the staff and board that either an addition/renovation to the current building or a new building was needed. As a result of the meetings with the city government, architects, and others, the city is currently renovating the 1902 Santa Fe depot building (over 22,000 square feet) to house both the public library and the local museum. The project is being funded by local fundraising efforts that have raised over $2 million in two years.

Communication was the key to success. The library staff and the board worked together at communicating to the community and city government the needs of the library. An extensive educational process was necessary to inform everyone of the library's present and future needs, the importance of the library in the community, and the potential for the new and improved services.

The entire project went well! While it is not yet complete, it appears that the library will have a beautiful and functional home. A local fundraising committee (consisting of board and local residents) has worked with a professional fundraising consultant to raise the necessary moneys without placing undue strain on the already busy library staff. At the same time, the staff have worked closely with the architects to design an interior that is functional.

Susan's advice to others contemplating a similar plan is: "Educate your community as to what a library is and should be before beginning the project. Unless they see that it will directly improve their lives, they will not support it. Hire a professional fundraising consultant. The first step must be a feasibility study to determine if the community will support the project financially. Also, get their advice on how to proceed."

SUMMARY
Few library endeavors involve as many people as erecting a new library building. If you are planning to build a new library, seriously consider the following recommendations:

1. Involve the entire community as much as possible.
2. Develop a plan based on community needs.
3. Hire professionals to do what they do best—planning, fundraising, and architecture. Don't be afraid to pay for their services; they are worth it.

4. Get realistic cost estimates—then add 10 percent.
5. Communicate! Communicate! Communicate! Let everyone know what you are doing as often as you can and in as many ways as you can.
6. Coordinate the efforts of various groups. Don't let one group keep the others in the dark.
7. Share the credit or, better yet, give it to others. It will make you look good.

CONDUCTING PUBLIC RELATIONS

WHAT IS GOOD PUBLIC RELATIONS?

Anything someone from your library does that creates better feelings about the library

WHAT IS BAD PUBLIC RELATIONS?

Anything that causes people not to use the library

Perhaps the most direct way to acquire fame is to affirm, confidently and persistently, and in every possible way, that we already have it.

Leopardi

All libraries have public relations. Whether they like it or not—whether it's good or bad, high-powered or low-key—all libraries have it. Unfortunately, for some libraries, it is often low-profile and seldom pushed far beyond the library itself.

Public relations is a proactive effort to create a positive image in the minds of the people about the library. Left alone, library public relations will suffer. Public relations is not something the librarian or the trustees do on their own. Library trustees should take the time to work with the librarian to create a good image for the library. Good public relations is ongoing, consistent with the goals of the library, coordinated with everything the library does, responsible and sensible. It is not a flash in the pan, self-serving, puffed-up, or false advertising. Good public relations take time.

When I first moved to South Carolina in 1971, I thought I would impress people by identifying myself as the *director* of the county library. A common response was, "Oh, that's nice. Where is the library?" Even though it was located in the heart of the retail district, the library was so invisible that most people didn't know where it was.

I had to increase visibility for the library, but before I could do that, I had to produce the programs people expected from a public library. It doesn't pay to advertise if you don't have the goods to back your advertising.

EFFECTIVENESS EQUALS IMAGE

Thomas Childers and Nancy Van House in their *Public Library Effectiveness Study* conducted a survey of community leaders, local officials, friends, trustees, users, library managers, and service librarians. All of these groups agreed that the following factors are important for library effectiveness:

- Convenience of hours
- Staff helpfulness
- Range of services
- Range of materials
- Services suited to community needs
- Materials quality

- Staff quality
- Materials availability
- Convenience of location
- Contribution to community well-being
- Managerial competence
- Awareness of service.

TIME FOR AN IMAGE CHECK

Are we doing a good job, but nobody knows it? That's why we have to take time to see ourselves as others see us. The person who asked me, "Where is the library?" gave me an outsider's window through which I could see the library.

If the image of your library is incorrect, you have to get outside the library to fix it. Changing public perception without getting out of the library is like taking a bath in a wet suit. You become so accustomed to the way you see your situation that you can't see it the way others do. You could have all kinds of videos, CDs, and the latest bestsellers, but if people think of your library as a warehouse of books, and the librarian as a baby-sitter of books, you will always have funding problems.

Stop! Take a minute right now to assess your library's image. How do people see it? How do you see it? Make a list of three things you could do next week that would make a difference in how the public sees your library. Write one of the ideas on your "To Do List" for next Monday.

Then do it.

Targeting public relations activities only to those who already come to the library is like preaching to the choir. They already know and love the library. You want to reach those who aren't aware of the benefits of the library, but are ready to be converted.

While the creation of publicity pieces is generally a staff duty, board members can do much to further the library's cause. A strong policy in support of public relations activities is a good place to start. Budget support for public relations activities is a necessity. Board members may have good writing skills, plus an "in" with the local newspaper editor. Exploit every opportunity to get the library's message before the public. Know what the message is and drive it home every chance you get.

FACE-TO-FACE CONTACTS

The best public relations is conducted face-to-face with people in the community. Trustees are naturals for this kind of image enhancement. People who feel good about the library will support it.

Here are some questions that can help focus and clarify a public relations effort:

- What is the purpose of the message? Inform, persuade.
- What is the direct benefit of the library's program to the audience?
- What are the convenient actions open to the public? Give money, volunteer, write, use it.
- What words or symbols are most likely to reach the target audience?
- How can togetherness and satisfaction be emphasized?
- What are the few main points the audience should remember?
- How can accomplishments be emphasized and failures be minimized?
- How will the audience respond to the message? Visualize the impact.

Library trustees will do their best public relations work in the supermarket, on the golf course, at social and community gatherings of all kinds. They will succeed as PR superstars if they are focused and understand the goals of the library.

PERFORMING WELL IS GOOD PR

Now take a look at your actual performance. Do your hours meet the needs of the community? Do you have the materials to give the people what they want when they come in? What about the staff? Are they friendly, helpful, and well-trained? What do you do if the library doesn't have the material requested?

How is your library perceived by the people in your community? Go through the Checklist for Library Image and Performance (Figure 9-1) to see how well you are doing.

FUNDRAISING AS A PR ACTIVITY

You may not believe this, but fundraising is good public relations. It raises the public's consciousness of the library. Trustees who are involved in a fundraising effort have many opportunities to promote the library. Think of the message you send to the community when you engage in fundraising: the library board is active; they care about the library; the library is good for the community. There are others. Why not make your own list?

Money is the obvious reason you do fundraising. You spend it and if you need more you go out and ask the people to give more.

FIGURE 9-1 Checklist for Library Image and Performance

	Yes	No	Suggested Action
1. Is the name of your library clearly visible from the street?	—	—	_____
2. Are library hours posted so they can be read by someone from the street?	—	—	_____
3. Is library parking adequate?	—	—	_____
4. Is library parking specially marked for short term parking?	—	—	_____
For the handicapped?	—	—	_____
5. Does the library have a curb-side book deposit for after-hours book-return?	—	—	_____
6. Do library grounds and exterior appearance meet or exceed community standards?	—	—	_____
7. Is the library accessible to the handicapped?	—	—	_____
8. Are library hours adequate to meet community needs?	—	—	_____
10. Is the library collection current and readily available?	—	—	_____
11. Do the books look new and inviting to the reader?	—	—	_____
12. Does the physical arrangement draw people in?	—	—	_____
13. Is the staff friendly and courteous?	—	—	_____
14. Is the staff knowledgeable and helpful?	—	—	_____
15. Is the library a nice place to be?	—	—	_____

Fundraising also creates a positive impact for tax initiatives. A good fundraising effort will spotlight your need and enhance your chances for increased tax support.

Early in 1988 the Great Bend Public Library solicited cash gifts through a letter explaining our dire financial circumstance. Every board member helped with the fund drive, which produced over $3,000. This effort focused the voters on our need. A few months later, when we asked them to approve a mill levy increase for the library, they did. The annual tax increase amounted to more than ten times the amount of our fundraising effort.

GOOD PR IN COLORADO

Lewis R. Burton, past president of trustees of the Pikes Peak Library District, Colorado Springs, says, "Great public relations was the key to the voters approving a bond issue and mill levy increase to build a major facility for the library. Every trustee was involved in selling the public on the need and services to be provided by the new library." His advice to others planning a similar project is to "present a positive image of the library and of the increased service to be provided."

Public relations is not solely the purview of the librarian or the board. It is possible for library staff to carry on a strong publicity campaign, advertising the programs and services of the library and attracting many people to come to the library. Trustees promote the library with their friends, but this is not all there is to public relations. Working together, trustees and library staff can create a total approach to public relations.

The Public Relations Planning Form (Figure 9-2) is designed to help you organize and implement a public relations activity.

Getting more people to use the library is a common goal of many trustees and librarians. Try running this idea through the PR Planning Form. The interesting thing about the process is that whatever you write on the form takes on a life of its own. If you can write it down, you can have it.

VISIBILITY IDEAS

Here are a few ideas for increasing the visibility of your library.

- Prepare a short video about the library. (Keep it to seven minutes or less.)

FIGURE 9-2 Public Relations Planning Form

1.   What is the mission statement for your library?

(See the Mission Statement in Appendix B)

2.   What library program or activity do you want to promote?

3.   What is your vision for the targeted program or activity?

4.   How does this program fit in the grand scheme of things at the library?

5.   What would you like to do?

6.   What are the alternatives?

FIGURE 9-2 *Cont'd.*

7.   What is the decision of the group?

8.   If (a) represents where you are today and number (j) represents where you want to be, what actions will you have to take to get there? Make your list, assign individuals to take action by certain dates in descending order.

	Task	Individual	Date
(a)			
(b)			
(c)			
(d)			
(e)			
(f)			
(g)			
(h)			
(i)			
(j)			

9.   How will you follow up to make sure the tasks get done on time?

10.   How will you evaluate your success? (What does your vision say about your success?)

- Offer to present programs for civic groups (with or without the video).
- Visit schools, clubs, and church groups. Offer the opportunity to sign up for a library card. Send a welcoming letter with each library card.
- Try Dial-A-Story for children. Be sure to get an easy telephone number for children to remember and dial.
- Set up a brown-bag book review or film program during the lunch hour. Offer coffee or tea.
- Team up with the fire department, home extension, or chamber of commerce to do a program of mutual interest. You get to share information with each others constituents.
- Sponsor contests—photography, poetry, posters, or reading, just to name a few. You will attract lots of new people to the library.
- Promote an annual event. The Great Bend Public Library sponsors a Poetry Rendezvous the first Sunday in August. It has become a special event for poets across the country.
- Publish a monthly newsletter. Send it to local business and government leaders. Tell them how the library can help them and how much money they can save by using the library.
- Hold story hours for children in unique locations—places where they get together informally. Day care centers have a ready-made audience. Their directors will love you. (Adapted from my article "New Visibility for the Small Public Library," *Wilson Library Bulletin,* January 1977.)

Most of these ideas reach people where they are and where they congregate. It is foolish for us to expect the general public to see the library as a librarian sees it. Yet how often do we see our librarians stuck behind a desk, just waiting for the public to recognize our great worth?

Trustees don't need to take a back seat to the librarian on any of these activities. Trustees can give book reviews, help with story hours, judge contests—even read poetry.

SUMMARY

Public relations is the image you or someone from the library conveys to the public. The message is always positive or negative; it is never neutral. It is the trustee's responsibility to see that the image is as positive as it can be.

Do people get what they want when they come to your library? If so, you will probably have the support you need to get the funding you need. Sometimes we have to see ourselves through the eyes of others to become aware of our shortcomings. The self-assessment tests in this chapter will help you see your library more clearly.

In order for the library public relations program to be effective, it must be well planned, well organized, and well funded, with plenty of staff support and help from individual board members.

We can try to see ourselves as others see us. Greater visibility will come when librarians and trustees go beyond the walls of their offices or board rooms and into their communities. If librarians and trustees will broaden their horizons, and never give up, the library's image will improve.

10 PLANNING FOR THE FUTURE

*Strategic planning is worthless unless there
is first a strategic vision.*

John Naisbitt

Planning is intellectual creation. We create our own future by envisioning it first and then setting the course to make it happen. The key to success is to visualize the accomplishment clearly. Make it realistic, yet challenging. Make it measurable and set a completion date.

Vision is the heart and soul of every project. What is your vision for your library? If every member of your team has the same vision for the library and you are willing to work together, there is no reason for your plan to fail.

You want people to get what they want when they come to your library. However, they may not be able to do that with things the way they are now. Perhaps you are stuck in a library that was built in 1912 with a grant from Andrew Carnegie. The elderly and the disabled in the community can't climb the eleven steps to the front door. If they could get inside, they would find it so crowded they could barely turn around. If that is the way it is, it is time to plan for something better. Albert Einstein said, "The significant problems we face cannot be solved at the same level of thinking we were at when we created them."

You want more for your library than a roof that doesn't leak and a warm place for people to come in winter. You want to expand the vision of your community through high-tech equipment and up-to-date materials. Children are using computers every day—not as toys, but as tools to gain speedier access to information. You want more for your library so it can reach more people in the community. It will take a higher level of thinking to accomplish the goal.

THE POWER OF GOAL SETTING

Why not shoot for the moon?

President John Kennedy set the vision for NASA in a speech given on May 25, 1961, when he said, "This nation should commit itself to achieving the goal, before this decade is out, of landing a man on the moon and returning him safely to earth." The task before you may seem just as awesome. You can accomplish it, just as NASA did. If you can write it down, you can have it.

What happens when we write down a goal like raising $500,000?

129

The problem is turned over to the subconscious mind, which works on it without conscious effort. Things fall into place. We meet people. We read something or write it. Thoughts come to our mind. Everything moves us steadily towards our goal.

PLANNING FOR GROWTH IN OREGON

Brian Diehm, a library trustee in Lake Oswego, Oregon, tells how planning for growth benefited the library:

> The board and director observed growth in demand for library service and foresaw the inadequacy in the near future of the four-year-old library building. Nobody in town wanted to believe that. The board and director convinced a reluctant city council to appoint a citizen task force to plan growth of the library. With the help of the city manager, the board mapped out a charge for the task force. One board member and the director served on the task force, to keep things "on track" with facts, statistics, and research.
>
> The key to success was the involvement of board and director working together to overcome citizen and council reluctance. Incorporating other citizens in the team, we thought of ourselves (board, task force, director) as a team.
>
> We developed a document that clearly maps out how library growth should occur, to provide the levels and types of services the citizens want. We now are ready, with a new director, to move into implementation, including a major fundraising campaign. We have the city council on our side now, thanks to the task force report. The only thing we would do differently is to carry out more detailed planning, so that when we took it to the public, it would be a complete package, a fully detailed vision.

Their advice to others is: "Reach out to every sector of your community. Realtors, city planners, bankers, lawyers, movers and shakers—all can help in the task. Enlist them as allies. You will be visiting them all later for money. If they have already helped, they are already committed. Financial commitment is then a short step for them to take."

Your goal may not be as lofty as putting a man on the moon, raising $500,000, or writing a book. It may be as simple as carpeting the children's room of the library. Can you see the carpet? What color is it? Can you feel the texture? Can you experience its softness under your feet? Can you see children lying on it, reading? If you can, you can have it. If you can get others to catch the same vision, you can have it sooner. The key to planning is creating a vision and having other people share it.

Once, while conducting a workshop, I asked Sandy Shields, a library trustee from Minneapolis, Kansas, about her vision for her library. She said, "I see a brand new library."

I asked, "What does it look like? What does it have in it?"

She said, "I see two rest rooms. One for women and one for men—both accessible to the handicapped."

"What else do you see?"

She said, "I see a comfortable, quiet place to sit and read magazines."

I pursued her vision for the library with her and she told me more of what she saw. Then I said, "If you can write it down, you can have it." Somehow putting it down on paper changes the level of commitment. The difference between a wish and a goal is a number and a date—written down on paper.

THE PLANNING PROCESS

Let's look at planning as a process. There are many good books on planning, and you can find them. One of the best I have seen is: *Managing Change: A How-To-Do-It Manual for Planning, Implementing and Evaluating Change in Libraries* by Susan C. Curzon. If you will plug your library project into the model she uses and work together, you will be successful. Another good book on library planning is *Planning and Role Setting for Public Libraries: A Manual of Options and Procedures*, prepared for the Public Library Development Project (American Library Association). It has work forms, checklists and charts to help you plan for your library.

ALA PLANNING PROCESS: A SUCCESS

Lynde M. Lee, Director of the Calcasieu Parish Library in Lake Charles, Louisiana, tells of a successful experience using the planning process mentioned above.

We undertook the ALA/PLA Planning process with the following results:

1. A five-year plan for the development of resources and

services for the determination of primary and secondary roles for each branch;

2. a comprehensive capital improvement plan for the upgrading of facilities necessary to provide the resources and service included in this five-year plan;
3. an automation project to provide an integrated online library automation system;
4. successful passage of a referendum to provide $12 million for capital improvements and doubling of operating revenues to improve services.

Board involvement has continued through the capital improvement program. Board members are serving on the project planning team with architects, staff, and consultants. Board attendance at meetings has increased to almost 100 percent. Individual members are becoming more active, and staff are growing more comfortable with trustees, seeing them as co-workers and not just aloof powers.

The key to our success was using the planning process to determine what our community wanted and needed in library services now and for the next five years. The board and staff are both working for the same objectives. Both know what those objective are and see us as a team working together. The board is more enthusiastic about their responsibilities as board members and feel more keenly their obligations to the public.

Aspects that went well include:

1. Everyone was on an equal basis without rank (first names were used).
2. Public input and involvement was high.
3. A good consultant was hired to help organize and facilitate the process.
4. The adopted plan reflects the wants and needs of the public.

If we had to do it again, this is what we would do differently: ask for more funds for capital improvements. Some sacrifices were made in order keep the amount of the bond issue as low as possible due to the fear that the issue wouldn't pass. Despite depressed economic conditions, voters approved the issue by a 73 percent majority. Approval didn't come because of the amount, but because of the planning and accountability.

Their advice to others is: "Be open minded and be willing to accept the results of the planning process. Board and public involvement has to be genuine, not tokens. Trustees and community representatives will work as hard and be as dedicated as library staff if they are truly involved and valued. Dare to dream; don't underestimate the public and their commitment to libraries."

PLANNING WITH A PURPOSE

The purpose of planning is to organize, manage and control change in a way that meets the needs of the organization. The first job of any planning group is to assess the current need. You do this by asking: Where are we now? What are our concerns? What is occurring? To whom? How often? So what? Does it really matter? Your job is to figure out what matters most in your library and do something about it.

In 1989 I sat down with the department heads of the Great Bend Public Library for an all-day session to plan for the future of the library. Afterwards we shared the following summary with the board and some community leaders:

Our library is:

—An inviting place to work.
—A neat place to be.
—Friendly.
—Filled with books.
—Roomy and pleasant.
—Free and open.
—Clean.
—An information place.
—Relaxing at times.
—Busy.
—Spacious.
—For every one.
—Comfortable.
—Impressive.

When people come to our library they think:

—It is a nice place.
—It's got a lot of services I didn't know about.
—It's very impressive.
—Staff members were helpful and friendly.
—It's a busy place.

Our library should be:

—Helpful.
—A friendly place where people will feel welcome and at ease.
—User-friendly (easy for patrons to use by themselves).
—Inviting.
—A vital community resource.
—Peaceful.
—Active in community life.
—Necessary.

I wish we could fix:

—Clutter around the circulation desk.
—Clutter in all work areas (not housekeeping).
—More up-to-date information.
—Signage (directional signs and location of various services).
—Broken chairs and tables.
—The "What's Happening Board."
—More recreational reading.
—Videos in a new location.

Our patrons generally fit into the following categories:

—Recreational readers.
—Those who need occasional information.
—Researchers:

    1. Students from kindergarten through college.
    2. Genealogy, family history.
    3. Business (stock market).

Our primary target audience is the pre-school child and the out-of-school adult:

—We do a fairly good job of serving the research needs of students K-12, though we could use more help from the teachers. Our most glaring gap is meeting research needs of college students.
—How do we impress the colleges that they are responsible for meeting the library needs of their curriculum?
—Tentative mission statement: "Our business is to meet the knowledge, information, and reading needs of the people."

—We wanted to have a mission statement that people could remember easily.

Categories of needs:

"More Books and Materials:
—Current reference material
—More recreational reading
—Books talked about on TV
—Replacement of lost or stolen books
—Books on tape
—Collection evaluation.
General appearance (physical plant):
—Signage
—Asbestos removed
—Enough chairs for tables
—Office space
—Space utilization
—New place for videos
—Borrower application card files
—New carpet
—Reupholster chairs
—Window treatments
—Lighting system
—Add third floor.
Public awareness:
—Outdoor signage: 2 1/2-foot brown letters on white stone northeast side of building.
—Change address on all publicity pieces to read: "Broadway and Williams"
—Distribute more information outside of library.
—Write a new brochure
—Create a packet of information for new borrowers
—Piggyback with other groups.
Public access to collection without help from staff:
—Signage—labels
—Card catalog sign up-to-date
—Bibliographic instruction (information on how to use the library)
—Map of where things are in the library
—Location of special collections
—Public access catalog—computer
—Space considerations.
Streamline circulation process:

—Automated checkout and return
—Bibliography generator
—Borrower registration
—Overdue books
—Holds
—Borrower inquiry (What books do I have checked out?)
—Inventory control
—On-order file
—Automatic stop on delinquent borrowers
—Statistical analysis of use of collection.

From the list of needs we created two lists of objectives:

1. We can do it now—in the next six months with little or no outside help (see Figure 10-1).
2. Long-term objectives requiring help and/or additional funding (see Figure 10-2).

The criteria for good objectives are:

—What is going to be done, specifically?
—Who is going to do it?
—What is the date for its completion?
—How can we measure if it has been done or not?

This was the first phase of the process. Most of the "do it now" goals were accomplished. Most of the goals with dollars attached to them are still waiting for the budget crunch to pass. But the fact that we wrote them down made them concrete, achievable aims.
You could use this same process and make it work for your library.

SETTING PRIORITIES

A key to accomplishing the goal is the way you prioritize your action plan. For each possible action ask the following questions and limit your answers to those offered here:

1. Can we, as a group, control the events?
   a. Yes, completely.
   b. Yes, but we will need some help.
   c. No.
2. How great will the impact be?
   a. A major step forward.
   b. A moderate step forward.
   c. A minor step forward.

The answers to these two questions can help you decide whether or not to proceed with the project. Let's take an example through the model. Suppose you want to raise $300,000 to build a new library. The action you are considering is to go for a bond election. Ask yourself this question: Can we as a group control the events of a bond election? The answer could be b or c. Then ask: What will be the scope of the effect? It will be a major step forward—a. If you have a good chance for success, go for it.

You might have the situation where the action would be a minor step forward and your group cannot control the situation. Forget it. Move on to an action that has a better chance for success. If you want to do something where your group controls the events completely and it will be a major step forward, go for it. What are you waiting for? Do it today!

This is the way to rank your actions:

1-a; 2-b (Group controls event, moderate step forward).

1-b; 2-a (Group needs help, major step forward).

1-b; 2-b (Group needs help, moderate step forward).

If your group controls the action, even if it is a moderate step forward, it should become a priority because your chance of success is very high. If you have to rely on the help of others, your success is not guaranteed.

After completing a Project Action Form (see Figure 10-3) for each idea, you can arrange them according to starting date. Since some actions may depend on others, they will have to be done first. For example: if want to close the street in front of the library so you can have a craft fair, you need city council approval to close the street. You have to have that approval before you can move ahead with your planning. Your project planning has to include the names of the person in charge and those who will be called upon to help. In this case, each board member may be called on to contact a council member before making the formal presentation.

No project is ever complete until the evaluation is done. It helps to establish the evaluation criteria beforehand. Ask yourself, "How will I know if it works?" and "When will I know?" This helps to fix the vision mentioned earlier in this chapter.

After the project is completed two popular questions are: "What went well?" and "What could we do differently to make it more successful next time?"

Indeed, this was the way the NASA finally put a man on the moon. They learned from every Apollo mission—even the ill-fated Apollo XIII mission. Planning helps us to learn from every experience—even the ones we consider failures. Creating the strategic vision turns the process over to our subconscious, which in turn

---

FIGURE 10-1 Do It Now (In the Next Six Months) List

8/8/89	Put "Williams and Broadway" as address for publicity	Terri, all
8/15/89	Revise Assignment Alert Packets	All
9/1/89	Update range cards	Kathy, Terri
9/9/89	Complete revision of procedures manual	All
9/15/89	Clear up clutter in work areas and circulation desk and reference desk	All
10/1/89	Make bibliographic instruction signs for top of card catalog	TC,KM,SD
10/1/89	Create procedure for handling set up for programs	Jim, Leo
11/1/89	Develop packet for new borrowers	Terri, all
11/1/89	Fix chairs for reading room	Leo
11/1/89	Print a new brochure, outlining library services	Terri, Jim, all
11/1/89	Update bibliography for working with other groups	Kathy, Jan
1/1/90	Complete adult materials inventory	Kathy, Debbie Rains
1/1/90	Complete inventory of children's department	Sandy, Cindy
1/1/90	Conduct space utilization study	All
1/1/90	Install the word "LIBRARY" in two-foot high brown letters on white concrete northeast side of library	Friends
1/1/90	Make covers for microform readers	Jim
1/1/90	Paint maintenance work room	Leo
1/1/90	Update card catalog (re-do nonfiction cards)	KM & DR

(Assigning names and dates for accomplishment is a key to realizing the goal.)

FIGURE 10-2 Future Objectives

6/1/90	Develop signage plan	All
1/1/91	*Install new signage	$5,000
1/1/92	*The book budget will equal $75,000	$25,000
1/1/91	*Automated circulation system ready for installation	$100,000
1/1/95	*Add 5,000 square feet to library building. (third floor)	$500,000
1/1/91	Add four more story hours	$10,000
1/1/91	Add two (circulation and acquisition) clerks	$20,000
1/1/91	Install window treatments	$1,500
1/1/92	Add one reference librarian	$20,000
1/1/92	Increase periodical budget to equal $10,000	$3,000
1/1/92	Plan for minimum wage increase	$10,000
1/1/95	Add (replace) furniture	$50,000
1/1/95	Cover (paint) asbestos	$30,000
1/1/95	Install new carpet	$50,000
	Total	$831,500

* Top priority.

FIGURE 10-3 Project Action Form

Project Name: _____

What do you want to do? Be very specific.

What are the driving forces? Who or what is working for you?

How will you put these forces to work for your project?

What are the restraining forces? Who or what can work against you to keep you from reaching your objective?

What can be done to deal with restraining forces?

Who will be the key person in charge of this project? (Write the name here.)

Who are the others who must be involved? (Write their names here.)

When will this project begin? _____

When will it end? _____

When the project is completed, what will the results look like? (Describe the project successfully completed.)

FIGURE 10-4 Activity Planning Guide

Activity_____

Leader_____

Purpose_____

When (Date and Time)_____

Who is invited_____

Members of planning committee_____

Resources needed:

      Human_____

      Financial_____

      Material_____

Tasks to do (assignments)	Responsible Person	Date
1._____	_____	_____
2._____	_____	_____
3._____	_____	_____

Post Activity Evaluation:

How well was the purpose of the activity accomplished?

Who was impacted?

How were they affected?

Who attended, who did not attend?

What were the highlights?

What are the recommendations for doing the activity better?

_____

_____

brings people, things, and ideas to us that will help us reach our goal.

PLANNING SPECIFIC ACTIVITIES

You may not be planning a grandiose project for the 21st century, but simply need to plan the next trustee training session; the Activity Planning Guide in Figure 10-4 may help you.

SUMMARY

Whether you are building a new library or conducting a new trustee orientation session, planning is crucial to you success. Take the time to organize, work your plan, and then evaluate your success.

If the librarian has a key role in making the plan work, then he or she must help with the planning. It is the best way secure the "buy in" so critical to success.

Martin Luther King, Jr. was another visionary of our time. His "I Have a Dream" speech made on August 28, 1963, set the vision for the future of the civil rights movement in America. He outlined his dream for the future of the United States when all people will live and work together in peace and be judged by the content of their character and not by the color of their skin.

Sometimes our libraries require such visionary people. What *is* your vision for your library? Are you the one who will stand up and say, "I have a dream for our library"? Can you see what it will be like when your dream is realized?

Remember! Every good plan starts with a vision. Whether it is putting a man on the moon or making a rest room accessible to the handicapped, it starts in the mind of the person who dares to put it down on paper. You start by writing your vision down and then sharing it with others. Then work together to achieve it.

APPENDIXES

Now that you have finished *Working Together*, take a few minutes to think about what you have learned. Use the Action Plan in the introduction to jot down a few ideas you think will help your library. Review the material in the appendix. The sample documents will help you formulate plans for your own library.

APPENDIX A

CITIZEN'S REQUEST FOR RECONSIDERATION OF A BOOK

Author: _____ Hardcover _____ Paperback _____

Title: _____

Publisher (if known): _____

Request initiated by: _____

Telephone: _____ Address: _____

City: _____ State: _____ Zip: _____

Complainant represents: _____ Self _____ Organization (name: _____

1. To what in the book do you object? (Please be specific. Cite pages.) _____

_____

2. What do you feel might be the result of reading this book? _____

_____

3. For what age group would you recommend this book? _____

_____

4. Is there anything good about this book? _____

_____

5. Did you read the entire book? If not, what parts did you read? _____

_____

6. Are you aware of the judgment of this book by literary critics? _____

_____

7. What do you believe is the theme of this book? _____

_____

8. What would you like the library to do about this book? _____

_____

9. In its place, what book of equal literary quality would you recommend that would convey the same picture and perspective of our civilization?

_____

Signature of Complainant   Date of Complaint

_____   _____

This matter will be considered by the Library Board of Directors and the Librarian.

APPENDIX B

PUBLIC LIBRARY POLICIES: GUIDELINES AND SAMPLES

Guidelines: Statement of purpose or mission statement

Every library, regardless of size, should have a mission statement, which is the beginning statement of their policy and by-laws. It should tell the reader what the library wants its services to be.

Sample Mission Statement

The Central Public Library is in business of educating, informing and meeting the recreational needs of the people in the community. It supports life-long learning with special emphasis on educational activities for pre-school children and out-of-school adults. The staff strives to give the people what they want when they come to the library.

Our Library's Mission Statement:

TRUSTEE BY-LAWS

Guidelines: Board Meetings

The library board should meet on a regular basis. Monthly meetings are preferable. Most states have an open meeting law that requires all library board meetings to be open to the public. The librarian should attend every board meeting unless his or her performance or salary is being discussed. Even then, some states require that the librarian be present.

The board meeting should be at the convenience of the members of the board. Meeting times can be changed as the composition of the board changes. A person should not be kept from serving on the board just because he or she cannot attend the meeting at the time it is currently scheduled.

You also need a provision for special meetings with proper notification to comply with the open meetings law.

Sample Policy: Board Meetings

The library board will meet the second Tuesday of each month at 7:30 p.m. in the library. Special meetings may be called at the request of the president of the board and/or the library director for the purpose of discussing urgent library matters with notification to the local newspaper 36 hours before the time of the meeting.

Our Library Policy: Board Meetings

Guidelines: Election of officers

Each year the library should designate a portion of a regular meeting for the purpose of electing officers. This is usually done after new members have been appointed to the board. The officers to be elected are President, Vice-President, Secretary, and Treasurer.

Sample Policy: Election of officers

The election of officers will be held during the May meeting each year. Officers to be elected are President, Vice-President, Secretary, and Treasurer. All officers will serve for one year with the option of being re-elected the following year.

Our Library Policy: Election of officers

Guidelines: Annual Report

Every librarian should prepare an annual report for the board and community. This can be a terrific public relations piece. State libraries often require a statistical report each year. This report could be the basis for an annual report that you prepare for the community and the governing body.

Sample Policy: Annual Report

The library will provide an annual report as required by the State Library and it will serve to inform the governing body and the people in the community of library activities.

Our Library Policy: Annual Report

Guidelines: Duties of officers

The duties of each office should be outlined specifically in the by-laws or policy so that when individuals are elected to offices on the board they can turn to the guidelines and see exactly what is expected of them.

Sample Policy: Duties of officers

President:

1. Prepares the agenda for the board meeting with the librarian.
2. Presides at the board meetings and maintains order.
3. Expedites business in a manner compatible with the rights of those present.
4. Summarizes the discussion to clarify what has been said and to keep things moving toward closure.
5. Calls for motions at appropriate times.
6. Signs checks and other documents as necessary.
7. Appoints appropriate committees as needed.

Vice-President:

1. Presides in the absence of the president.

Secretary:

1. Maintains a record of the proceedings of all board meetings.
2. Reads the minutes of the last meeting (if required by the group).
3. Signs the minutes after they have been approved by the board.
4. Signs checks and other documents with the president as necessary.
5. Calls the meeting to order in the absence of the president or vice-president. The first item of business will be the election of a temporary president for the meeting.

Treasurer:

1. Keeps an accurate account of all financial transactions and makes a report to the board as necessary.
2. Signs checks and other documents as necessary.

Note: The librarian or another staff member may be designated by the board to be the recording secretary and that person may take the minutes and transcribe them for the board. Nevertheless, the secretary of the board is still legally responsible for maintaining a record of proceedings of all board meetings.

Note: The library board may delegate the record-keeping function of the treasurer to the librarian, bookkeeper, or other qualified accountant and pay for these services. The treasurer shall receive no compensation for fulfilling these duties.

Our Policy: Duties of Officers

Guidelines: Committees

Small committees can expedite the work of the board. Murphy's first law of meetings is, "The efficiency of a meeting is in inverse proportion to the number of people present." His second law of meetings is, "The duration of a meeting increases as the square of the number of people present." Keep your committees small! Your deliberations will be shorter and more efficient.

To keep the board from violating open meetings law, the number of people on a committee should always be less than the majority of a quorum of the full board. This means a board consisting of seven members should have committees of three members or less. On a board of five people committees should be just two people.

Regardless of the number of committees or their size, the librarian should staff the meetings to provide information for decision-making.

Sample Policy: Committees

The library will establish standing committees as follows: budget committee, planning committee, and publicity committee. These committees will be appointed each year by the incoming president. The librarian will be present at all committee meetings.

Our Library Policy: Committees

Guidelines: Requirement for a quorum

A quorum of the body is defined in the by-laws or policy. It is the minimum number of the group present at a meeting to conduct business—usually a majority of the members. Because most library boards are official guardians of public funds, it would be unwise to establish a quorum at less than a majority of the membership.

Sample Policy: Requirement for a quorum

A quorum shall be a majority of the members of the board and is required for the transaction of official business.

Our Library Policy: Requirement for a quorum

Guidelines: Board meeting agendas

The agenda of each board should be developed by the librarian and/or the President of the board. It should have a standard format that should include roll call, the reading of and/or approval of the minutes if they have been mailed in advance of the meeting, approval of the financial statement and of the monthly expenditures.

The usual motion for the payment of bills in a library board meeting is to "approve the monthly expenditures and to file the financial statement for the auditors." The meeting proceeds with the librarian's report, and any committee reports, correspondence, and special presentations. After that follows unfinished business, new business, the time and date of the next meeting, and adjournment.

Sample Policy: Board Meeting Agendas

The library director will work with the board president to create the agenda for each meeting. The planned agenda will be mailed to each board member and supplied to the local newspaper at least two days before the scheduled meeting.

Our Policy: Board Meeting Agendas

Guidelines: Parliamentary procedure

The library should follow Robert's Rules of Order. The library may elect to follow special procedures for small groups.

Sample Policy: Parliamentary procedure

The library will conduct all business according to Robert's Rules of Order where they are not in conflict with the policies that are adopted by this board. The library board meetings will be conducted under the Robert's Rules of Order Special Parliamentary Procedures for Small Groups.

Our Library Policy: Parliamentary procedure

Guidelines: Conflict of interest

A surefire way to get in trouble as a library trustee is to engage in a conflict of interest. Most states have conflict of interest laws for public officials. If you have a substantial interest in a business that could sell something to the library, using your influence on the board to make the sale is a conflict of interest. The best thing you can do is to find out what the law in your state says and draft your policy to conform to the law.

Sample Policy: Conflict of interest

No board member or staff member may engage in commerce with the library in a way that can be construed to be a conflict of interest. A conflict of interest is defined as any commercial activity that would enhance the wealth of the individual (other than employment or reimbursement for legitimate expenses) by virtue of influence he or she may have with the library. Exceptions to this include sealed bids through the normal bidding process and businesses that offer a product or service for which there is no competition within the service area of the library.

Our Library Policy: Conflict of interest

TRUSTEE POLICIES

Guidelines: Board relationship to librarian and staff
The library board should establish a policy that outlines the relationship between the board, the librarian, and other library staff members. This section should establish the responsibilities of the board and the duties of the librarian. Generally the library board has the responsibilities of setting policy, hiring a librarian, establishing the budget, monitoring the financial aspects of the library, and promoting public relations. The librarian usually has administrative functions in executing programs and the policies as directed by the board, assisting with the budget preparations, supervision of staff, etc. It is important that these relationships be set forth in policy so that, in the event of misunderstandings, the policy will take precedence.

Sample Policy: Board relationship to librarian and staff
The Board shall formulate and adopt all policies. The Librarian shall be charged with creating procedures to administer the policy and supervise the staff. The librarian will work with the board to develop the budget, conduct public relations, engage in planning, and review policies.

Our Library Policy: Board relationship to librarian and staff

Guidelines: Policy review
The library board should review the policies each year, checking for possible changes, additions, or editorial corrections. It is not necessary that the policy be changed every year, but board members should review the policy to re-acquaint themselves with that policy.

Sample Policy: Policy review

The library board and/or a committee appointed by the board president will review the policies of the library board each year during the months of September and October.

Our Library Policy: Policy review

Guidelines: Financial audit

An audit tells members of the board if the library funds have been spent according to the financial reports submitted by the treasurer or librarian. It also assures board members that library money was spent strictly for approved library purposes. Some states require all public agencies to have an audit. The library should have a financial audit conducted annually by a qualified public accountant. Some small libraries may not be required to have a financial audit because of their size, but one should be performed anyway, even if it is done by someone other than the treasurer of the board.

Sample Policy: Financial audit

The library will have a financial audit performed each year by a Certified Public Accountant.

Our Library Policy: Financial audit

Guidelines: Continuing education for trustees

The library should encourage board members to attend continuing education activities, including library association meetings. Wherever possible, the library should pay for all or at least part of the travel expenses for board members to attend these activities.

Sample Policy: Continuing education for trustees

The library encourages board members to attend continuing education opportunities—especially system workshops and state library conferences. The library will pay $.25 per mile for attendance at continuing education functions approved by the library board.

Our Library Policy: Continuing education for trustees

Guidelines: Physical plant
The library should maintain the physical facilities in a proper manner. The library policy should define who is responsible for maintaining the physical facilities.

Sample Policy: Physical plant
It shall be a responsibility of the librarian to see that the library is maintained in good physical condition. She or he is to make recommendations to the board for annual physical facilities projects and report maintenance needs.

Our Library Policy:

Guidelines: Insurance
The library board should maintain insurance on the building and the contents. Some cities will pay for the insurance on the library because the city owns the library. The library should insure the contents if the city doesn't. This insurance policy should be reviewed annually and revised to meet the needs for replacement costs of materials in the library and the cost of replacing the building.

Sample Policy: The library will maintain an insurance policy in force on the building and contents equal to 85 percent of the replacement costs.

Our Library Policy:

Guidelines: Use of meeting rooms
If the library has a meeting room, it should establish policies that govern its use and the conduct of the people who use it. This policy should include the concept that the meetings in the meeting room should be open to the public, free of charge. It should also establish

whether or not smoking will be allowed, whether or not food should be served, who is responsible for cleaning up the room, and whether or not meetings of a regular nature may be held in the room, i.e. every Thursday at 7:30 p.m.

Sample Policy: Use of meeting rooms

The library meeting room will be open for use by any not for profit club, group, or organization in the community that needs a place to meet. Meetings in the library meeting room shall be open to all members of the community without charge. Closed meetings will not be allowed. Food and beverages may be served in the meeting room. Cleanup will be the responsibility of the organization using the meeting room.

Our Library Policy: Use of meeting rooms

Guidelines: Friends of the Library

The Friends of the Library can be an asset to any library if the town is large enough to support such an organization. Friends form a solid advocacy group that can increase the library's visibility. They can also be a formidable fundraising group. Friends have traditionally raised funds for projects or acquisitions in excess of the general library budget.

The benefits of organizing a Friends of the library are not limited to fundraising. Here are a few other reasons you might want to organize a friends group:

- Volunteer service
- Help with passage of a bond issue or tax referendum
- Lobbying the legislature or city government
- Public relations
- Programming for the library
- A focal point for community support of the library.

Make sure you want a Friends group before you organize one. There is nothing more powerful for the benefit of your library than an active, well-directed Friends group. When the goals of the Friends coincide with the goals of the library, everything you set your hand to will succeed. The director, the board of trustees and a Friends group need to have the same focus—to assist the library in serving the community. However, it is essential that Friends cooperate with both of the other two but interfere with neither. Because of the independent nature of a Friends group, it can often undertake projects that far exceed the scope of trustees or staff. The library board, the director, and Friends need to work together to set priorities and define roles for the good of the library.

Many libraries provide office space for the Friends of the Library in addition to occasional clerical support from the library staff.

Sample Policy: Friends of the Library

The Friends of the library is an integral part of the library. In order to encourage cooperation and assist the Friends, the Library will provide an office for the Friends of the library, postage for mailings, clerical staff when needed, and storage for space for the used book sale. The library director and the president of the board will meet regularly to coordinate efforts on behalf of the library.

Our Library Policy: Friends of the Library

LIBRARY SERVICE POLICY

Guidelines: Services

This is an important part of your policy manual. List all the services your library offers, which should include the lending of books, periodicals, tapes, records, art prints and audiovisual equipment. Everything your library offers to the public should be listed here. If there are any restrictions or special applications, include them in your policy statement.

Sample Policy: Services

The following are the services of the library: circulation of books, audiocassette, videocassettes, compact discs, records, art prints, and superannuated encyclopedias. Reference materials to be used in the library include, encyclopedias, auto repair manuals, family history research materials, including the International Genealogical Index and state census records, telephone directories, and medical references. The library serves as a community information and referral service. The library also provides, and answers to reference questions, assistance with research, library skills instruction, and story hour for preschool children, Other services include, reader advisory services, interlibrary loan laminating service, photocopy service, state legislative information, and service for the homebound.

Magazines do not circulate.

Our Library Policy: Services

Guidelines: Who may borrow materials

Generally, anyone who comes to the library may use library materials without registering and without charge. Typically, those who live in the taxing district of the library may borrow from the library without charge. Some municipalities have extended borrowing privileges to those who work in their town, whether or not they pay taxes there. Some libraries charge nonresident families as much as $100 per year for a borrowers card. Your policy should include the details for reciprocal borrowing.

Sample Policy: Who may borrow materials

Anyone who resides or pays property taxes within the city may borrow materials from the library free of charge.

Our Library Policy: Who may borrow materials

Guidelines: Borrower registration

Anyone who wants to borrow materials from the library should be required to register. It's about the only way the library has of knowing where to send an overdue notice or to recover books that have been checked out. Registration should be as simple as possible. Don't ask and extraneous questions on the form. Here are a few elements you will probably want to include:

Date
Name
Address
Telephones (daytime, evening)
School (for children)
Occupation and business address
Name of spouse
Parents name and address (for children)
Name and address of near relative (for adults)

City resident (yes or no)
County of residence.

I have always mailed new library cards to borrowers. It is a good way to verify the address they have given you. We send a welcoming letter with their card and stamp the envelope "Do Not Forward." About five percent of all new cards are returned to us by the Post Office because the address is wrong or the people have moved. It is a good way to protect library property.

Sample policy: Borrower registration

Those who wish to borrow materials from the library must register, using the form provided by the library. The library director will establish procedures for registering new borrowers. New borrowers with unverified addresses may have their borrowing privileges limited until they receive their permanent card in the mail.

Our Library Policy: Borrower registration

Guidelines: Confidentiality of patron records

Libraries that used to have borrowers sign their names on checkout card are now finding they can't do that because patron records are confidential. I suppose they could use a thick black felt tip pen to cover the names, but that doesn't seem very practical. Libraries that use this method need to find another way of checking out books while maintaining a record of who has the book. Whatever they decide to do must assure that patrons cannot know what books other people have read. Some libraries consider patron confidentiality another reason to install an automated circulation system. Be sure to check the technological implications of your policy before you implement one that relies on computers.

This issue has seen many changes in the past few years and will likely see more changes in the future. Your best guide for current information on patron confidentiality is ALA's Office for Intellectual Freedom, 50 East Huron, Chicago, IL 60611; (312) 280-4223. Or check with your state library or your attorney. Forty-four states have laws regarding the confidentiality of patron records.

ALA's Office for Intellectual Freedom has a Modular Education Program, which is a self-training program. It uses patron confidentially as a model for intellectual freedom issues.

Every effort should be made to protect patron records, including requiring the agency that is seeking the information to "show just cause" in a court.

Sample policy: Confidentiality of patron records

The library will maintain absolute borrower confidentiality. Except under a specific court order, staff members will not reveal information contained in the borrower registration file or file of books checked out. The library will assign each borrower a number and check out books based on that number.

Our Library Policy: Confidentiality of patron records

Guidelines: Service to students and schools

The library should establish a policy regarding support of school curricula. While many of the patrons of the public library are students working on assignments, specific services to students must be defined. Some libraries try to provide everything for students. Other libraries do not. Some libraries have stated that their top priority is to serve out-of-school adults and pre-school children. Some public library officials believe that schools should support their own curricula with adequate school libraries paid for with tax funds designated for schools. Whatever your library does regarding this matter is up to the library board, and it should be reflected in your statement of purpose at the beginning.

Sample Policy: Service to students and schools

The library serves all people in the community, including students, and will maintain warm and cooperative relationships with public schools in the area. However, it will not intentionally try to support the curriculum of any school, except as its materials meet the informational needs of the general public. The public library gives priority to the information and recreation needs of pre-school children and out-of-school adults.

Our Library Policy: Service to students and schools

Guidelines: Library hours

Although the library should be open for the convenience of the library users, don't neglect the needs of the staff. Library hours are tied very closely to available resources. If your budget is small, you may not be able to afford to be open very many hours. Your system or state library may have standards on the number of hours libraries of different sizes should be open. Don't forget evening and weekend hours. If you are only open when most people are at work, how will they be able to use your library?

Whenever possible, keep the library open the same hours every day. It is better to have the library open from noon till 6 p.m. Tuesday through Saturday, than to have morning hours one day and evening hours another day and different hours on Saturday.

Sample Policy: Library hours

The library will be open 12 noon to 9 p.m. Monday through Thursday and from noon to 5 p.m. on Friday and Saturday. The library is closed on Sunday.

Our Library Policy: Library hours

Guidelines: Holidays

The library board establishes policy for holidays. The personnel policy should have a statement clarifying whether or not staff members will be paid and if they will be allowed time off for special religious holidays or when the holiday falls on a day the library is not open.

Sample Policy: Holidays

The library will be closed in observance of the following holidays: New Year's Day, Martin Luther King Day, Memorial Day, Independence Day, Labor Day, Veterans Day, Thanksgiving Day, Christmas Eve Day, Christmas Day, and New Year's Eve Day. When a holiday occurs on a Sunday the library observes the holiday on the following Monday.

Our Library Policy: Holidays

Guidelines: Number of items loaned

Many libraries have to restrict the number of books one person may borrow at any one time. The only good reason to do this is limited resources of the library. A limit of ten books per person is not uncommon. A limit of two or three bestsellers or books on a single topic may also be appropriate. A policy restricting the number of books on a subject helps the library ration materials when an entire school class has the assignment to find information on a single topic. It may, however, keep people from getting what they want when they come to the library.

Limiting new borrowers with unverified addresses to one or two books on their first visit is a good idea—especially if the library has had a problem with transient borrowers in the past.

Sample Policy: Number of items loaned

The maximum number of books or materials one person may borrow at one time is ten items. New borrowers with unverified addresses may borrow one book at a time until they receive their permanent card.

Our Library Policy: Number of items loaned

Guidelines: Loan periods

Every library must establish the length of the loan period. A longer loan period will be more accommodating to the patron and will probably result in fewer overdue books. On the other hand, shorter loan periods will encourage the return of the materials. But if your loan period is three weeks or less, the staff will spend a lot of time doing telephone renewals. A standard loan period is three to four weeks, with one week for current bestsellers. Magazines and reference books occasionally may be checked out for two or three days, depending on the library. If you check out magazines, be prepared to lose some. Most libraries prefer to offer access to a photocopier instead.

Sample Policy: Loan periods

The library will check out materials for three weeks. Current bestsellers will be checked out for one week. The librarian will determine which material shall be checked out for three weeks and which shall be checked out for one week.

Our Library Policy: Loan periods

Guidelines: Restrictions on materials loaned

The library may want to restrict certain books from circulation, especially reference books, expensive art books, etc. The fewer the restrictions, the better. The purposes of restricting some materials is to preserve their value for the future or to have the material available for others who may come to the library and need the material. But whatever you do, don't restrict access to information.

Sample Policy: Restrictions on materials loaned

The library will not lend reference materials that are specifically marked "reference." The library director and department heads have the authority to allow an overnight loan of reference material to be checked out just before the library closes and returned right after the library opens the next morning.

Our Library Policy: Restrictions on materials loaned

Guidelines: Overdue fines

This is one of the most hotly debated issues of library service. There are good reasons for charging fines for overdue books, and there are good reasons for not charging fines. Each library board must decide what its policy will be. *The only reason for charging overdue fines is to get the books back.* Charges should be enough to insure that the books are returned on time. At the same time, the charges should not be punitive. The amount one patron considers reasonable, another will consider excessive. Some libraries have developed an overdue charge connected with a grace period. The overdue charge is approximately the cost of generating and mailing the overdue notice. This seems to be a reasonable way to handle overdue books. Too often it costs the library more to send an overdue notice than it collects in fines.

Sample Policy: Overdue fines

The library will charge patrons for materials that are kept overdue at the rate of $.10 per day. In no case shall the overdue charge exceed the cost of the book. Regardless of the amount of the fine, the book remains the property of the library.

Our Library Policy: Overdue fines

Guidelines: Damage to library materials

The borrower should be responsible for materials borrowed from the library, even if he or she allows the book to be damaged or misused. This could include "accidents" of spilled milk or letting a pet chew on it. Such accidents could be construed as negligence and the borrower could be held liable for the full cost of the book. Charges should not be punitive, but the library must protect its investment. The cost of replacement should be charged to the patron. These charges should be made at the retail cost of the book plus, if desired, a minimal cost for processing. Patrons sometimes feel that if they pay for the cost of the book they should get the damaged book. If you agree with that attitude, your library could become a bookstore. Someone who wanted a rare book could mark it up and pay for it. The library might not be able to replace the book.

Torn or scribbled-on pages in children's books are a little different. If the book is still usable, don't make the patron pay for the whole book. If a book has already been circulated 100 times, don't make someone pay for a torn out page. That book doesn't owe you anything, neither should the patron.

Sample Policy: Damage to library materials

All library patrons will be responsible for the books and other materials they borrow from the library. Patrons will be fined for willful or negligent damage to the materials. If damage makes the book unusable, the patron will be charged retail cost of the book plus $2 for processing. Books that have been damaged and paid for remain the property of the library.

Our Library Policy: Damage to library materials

Guidelines: Smoking

Smoking is a proven health hazard, and more and more states

now have laws prohibiting smoking in public places. Libraries must comply with the law. They should also be responsive to the needs of all people in the community. If possible, you should have a designated area where people can smoke without bothering other people, even though this solution is becoming increasingly less popular.

Sample Policy: Smoking

In consideration of the health of all employees and patrons, smoking is not permitted in the library.

Our Policy: Smoking

Guidelines: Book Selection

First of all, your book selection policy guides the staff in the selection and purchase of materials. It should include phrases like: "literary merit and scholarship," "physical format," "objectivity," "readability," "balance of subject area," "representing all points of view," and "all sides of controversial issues."

Some people believe that there are some books or other library material that no one should read or see. They will go to any extent to enforce their views on the library and others. A well-crafted statement will blunt their onslaught.

Book selection is one of the highest responsibilities of a library professional. Yet without a selection policy, he or she may be taking the library into a pit of quicksand. If you don't have a book selection policy or if you feel uneasy about the one you have, examine book selection policies from other libraries and write one that meets the needs of your library.

Sample Policy: Book Selection (See Appendix C)

Our Library Policy

Guidelines: Local History

Every library should have a local history collection. Every library can collect materials produced in, on, or about their own county. The public library will often be the only place that this material can be preserved and made available.

Sample Policy: Local history

The library will collect as much information as is available about the town of _____ and the county. We will make a special effort to have access to local newspapers, either in hard copy or microfilm, and provide these to researchers who request them.

Our Library Policy: Local history

PERSONNEL POLICY

In the face of rapidly changing employment law, trustees and the library director need to work together to make sure their policy is up to date and meets the needs of the staff and the demands of the law. The board should pay particular attention to the personnel policy because it represents the greatest exposure to risk. Poorly handled personnel matters have resulted in law suits that have cost individual board members money. A carefully worded policy, scrupulously administered, can save board members grief.

Employment law has undergone dramatic change in the past few years. It almost takes a lawyer to stay current with the changes. The courts have ruled that personnel policies are implied contracts. Therefore, don't make a statement in your personnel policy that you wouldn't want to have written into a contract. For example: don't refer to regular employees as "permanent" employees unless you are willing to give everyone you hire a lifetime job or give up your right to dismiss someone for good cause.

Everything employers do, from the minute they have an opening they want to fill until the employee's heirs are gone, has come under the scrutiny of the courts. You write personnel policy to protect the rights of the employees and the library. Don't put something in your policy that could come back to haunt you.

Guidelines: Employment application

Hiring practices have caused employers as much grief as the treatment they give employees after they get on the payroll. Even though you have the right to hire qualified applicants or not hire those who are unqualified, your application form has to be as free as possible of elements that would distinguish between protected groups and non-protected groups (i.e., based on race, religion, age, sex, national origin, or disability.) Questions on the applications must relate to the individual and the work he or she has done for others or will be doing for you. Don't ask the question if it doesn't relate to the job. That is why it is wise to have different application forms for various positions. (See sample Employment Application in Chapter 4)

You may also want to include the criteria for an applicant's being interviewed in your policy. You may also want to include in your policy special procedures for recruiting the library director.

Sample Policy: Employment application

All applicants for employment will complete the formal application form supplied by the library. Failure to answer the required questions or sign the application will be grounds for rejecting the application.

Qualified applicants who appear to best match the job requirements will be invited for an interview. Part of the interview will include a review of the job description, which the applicant must sign to be eligible for employment. All applicants for a given position may be required to take a test appropriate to the job requirements. Information about previous employment will be verified.

After all interviews for the position are conducted, any and all applications may be rejected; otherwise, the library will offer the position to the qualified applicant who best matches the job requirements. The rate of pay will be confirmed at the time the job offer is made.

Our Library Policy: Employment application

Guidelines: Personnel appointments

Failure to outline conditions for hiring new employees can lead to problems. You need to state clearly who has the authority to hire and under what conditions that person has the authority to hire.

Sample Policy: Personnel appointments

The Director is appointed by the Board. All other employees are appointed by the library director. Regular appointment is made only after six (6) months of probation. Vacancies may be filled either by hiring someone new or by transfer or promotion of current employees. The director may also make interdepartmental transfers involving two or more persons when no vacancies exist, or may approve such transfers if requested by employees. Current staff will be given first consideration for vacancies for which they are qualified.

Guidelines: Beginning employment

Everyone who is hired by the library has the right to know what is expected of him or her. Certain information should be given to the new employee the first day on the job. This information should include such items as a copy of the library's policy, including the personnel policy; a copy of the job description; an outline of the benefits and perquisite of the job; a schedule of paydays. Although this point may appear to be in the area of procedures, putting it in the policy makes it clear that your library is not trying to hide anything from its employees.

Sample Policy: Beginning employment

The first day on the job, all new employees will receive a packet of information about the library the policies, and the job. The packet will include copies of the following: the library policy, including the personnel policy; the job description for the position being filled by the new employee; and "Information for New Employees," (See Appendix D).

Guidelines: Employment conclusions

One of the most risky things a board can do is to affect an involuntary conclusion to employment. The only reasons for dismissing someone are well-documented poor performance, failure to perform the job as assigned, misconduct at work, or flagrant violations of the law. If a staff member steals the fine money or is arrested for driving under the influence while driving a library car, you can fire him or her. Even then you may end up in court.

Federal law has eliminated retirement because of age. In the case of older workers, you base the employment conclusion on diminished capacity (though that is difficult to document) or on mutually agreed-upon retirement. You can, however, change the job assignment, offer an incentive to retire, or mutually agree upon retirement conditions in advance of the event.

Sample Policy: Employment conclusions

An employee wishing to resign must do so in writing, using the form provided by the office. In order to leave in good standing, professional librarians and administrative personnel are asked to give at least one (1) month's notice; others are asked to give at least two (2) week's notice. All resignations must include the employee's reason for resigning. Persons who have resigned forfeit all rights as employees of the library, including staff grievance procedures.

Grounds for dismissal shall be: 1) misconduct on the job (e.g., drinking alcohol at work or sexual harassment); 2) inefficiency on the job (e.g., failure to meet production standards); 3) failure to perform on the job (e.g., not doing the job as outlined in the job description); or 4) failure to comply with provisions of the personnel policy.

If the library director considers an employee's performance unsatisfactory, he or she will warn the employee, pointing out where improvement is necessary and suggesting ways in which the employee may improve. If performance remains unsatisfactory after a two-week period, the director shall give the employee two weeks' notice of dismissal.

A regular member of the library staff, dismissed by the director, shall be notified of such dismissal in writing in person or via certified mail. If the employee wishes a hearing, such must be requested within seven days of receipt of the dismissal notice. A hearing before the Board and the director or a personnel committee of the board will then be scheduled with at least 14 days of elapsed time between the dismissal notice and such hearing. If they so desire, both sides, may have a limited number of witnesses at the hearing. If the decision that follows is one of dismissal, the employee's termination date will be recorded as that date on which the original dismissal notice was given. If the employee is cleared and/or reinstated by the hearing, the original dismissal notice will be considered a suspension for cause, and restitution of any unpaid salary and accumulated benefits will be made.

In cases where continued employment would be seriously detrimental to the employee or to the library, the director may effect an instant dismissal, with the letter of notification to be a formality following the action.

Guidelines: Nepotism
In the public sector, it is not enough to be honest; you have to avoid the appearance of dishonesty. It may seem unfair for the library director not to be able to hire a son or daughter to be a shelver in the library, but if it is not against the law where you live, it probably ought to be. This is a conflict of interest and should be guarded against.

Sample Policy: Nepotism
Employment of members of the immediate families of Board

members is prohibited. Employment of members of the immediate families of administrative personnel, even for hourly employment, is made only with prior approval of the Board.

Our Policy: Nepotism

Guidelines: Classification and pay scale.

Every library should have a well-defined pay scale for all employees. These guidelines should be set and administered objectively. The salary of the librarian and the staff should be set by the library board in accordance with the established pay scale, not on an individual basis. Library salaries should be commensurate with other jobs in the community. The normal percentage of salaries and benefits for all employees of a public library is usually between 55 percent and 70 percent of the total budget.

Sample Policy: Classification and pay scale.

The library will establish a classification and pay scale and will update it annually based upon the available funds. Salary is earned and paid monthly. No employee will be paid less than the minimum wage.

Our Library Policy: Classification and pay scale

Guidelines: Other monetary benefits

Health insurance and retirement benefits are an integral part of your compensation package. Other benefits may not be as tangible, but nonetheless should be spelled out in your policy.

Sample Policies: Other monetary benefits

The Library provides health insurance for full-time staff members. Library liability for the cost of this program is limited to the amount established by the Board. Family coverage is available through payroll deduction.

The library participates in the Kansas Public Employees Retirement System. All full-time and part-time regular employees working more than 1,000 hours per year become members of this retirement system after one year of employment, or immediately upon employment if they are current members of the retirement system.

Our Policy: Other monetary benefits

Guidelines: Staff development

Educational development of library employees is critical to continued success of the organization. Library personnel must regularly reassess their knowledge, skills and attitudes if they are to remain competent workers. The library is responsible for helping staff members meet the challenges of accelerated change by supporting continuing education activities.

Continuing education is lifelong learning, defined as any formal or informal learning experience that builds on previous education and experience. Activities include:

1. Professional association meetings and programs;
2. Graduate library school courses and programs;
3. System workshops;
4. Commercial workshops or seminars;
5. Local community college courses;
6. Regents-approved college and university courses and programs.

The library may help staff members to attend continuing education events in any or all of the following way:

1. Verbal encouragement;
2. Granting time off;
3. Paying registration fees;
4. Paying travel expenses;
5. Giving salary increases after a certain level of achievement.

Sample Policy: Continuing education

Staff members may apply to attend training events. Based on available funds and training needs of the staff member, one of the following options will be authorized:

1. Library work time with total expenses paid;
2. Library work time, but at personal expense;
3. Personal time, but at library expense;
4. Personal time (leave without pay) at personal expense.

Staff members may arrange their schedules with their supervisors to accommodate attendance at an approved event. All materials purchased by the library for a training event become the property of the library.

Our Library Policy: Continuing education

Guidelines: Part-time employees

Most libraries have part-time employees. In fact, some head librarians are part-time employees. Part-time employees usually are not granted the same benefits as full-time employees and usually are paid at a lower rate. If you do not treat part-time people the same way you treat full time employees, you need to state specifically in your personnel policy what you will do for part-time workers. A way to solve the question of benefits such as vacation, sick leave, and health insurance, is to pro-rate the benefit based on the number of hours the part-time employee is scheduled to work. Another way is to allocate no benefits to part-time employees.

Sample Policy: Part-time employees

All part-time employees working on an hourly basis will be paid at the end of the month. They receive no benefits except for paid holidays that occur on days they are normally scheduled to work.

Our Library Policy: Part-time employees

Guidelines: Volunteers
Your library probably needs all the good help it can get. Volunteers are a valuable asset to libraries. Indeed, some libraries are virtually run by volunteers. It is important that the regular employees not feel that their income is being eroded by the use of volunteers. In some cities union contracts prohibit the use of volunteers to reduce staff.

You may wish to protect volunteers with Worker's Compensation benefits in the event of an on-the-job injury. Check with your Worker's Compensation Insurance agent for details.

Sample Policy: Volunteers
The library will use volunteers wherever possible to assist the librarian in his or her task of operating the library. Volunteers will not be used to replace or reduce the hours of regular staff.

Our Library Policy: Volunteers

Guidelines: Work hours and schedule.
The policy should state what constitutes a normal working day. If your library uses flex-time, it should be stated here. The hours that the librarian is on duty should also be included.

Supreme Court rulings and changes in the law make it imperative that library employees not work more than 40 hours per week.

If they do, you have to pay them time and a half or give them time and a half off. Check the Code of Federal Regulations, Title 29, Part 541.

Sample Policy: Work hours and schedule

The librarian is expected to work when the library is open, up to 40 hours per week. Full-time employees work a 40-hour week subject to the flex-time guidelines. Flex-time is designed to give individual workers some flexibility and control in determining their work schedules. Employees may work more than eight hours in one day as long as the total per week does not exceed 40 hours. Exempt personnel, as defined by Title 29, Part 541 of the Code of Federal Regulations, may accrue and use bank time as schedules necessitates at the rate one for one. Non-exempt employees may be requested by the director to work overtime. When this occurs, they will be granted bank time at the rate of time and a half for every hour worked.

Each employee is expected to check in whenever entering the building and check out whenever leaving the building. Each employee will keep an accurate time card, which will be turned in to the office at the end of each work week.

Our Library Policy: Work hours and schedule

Guidelines: Breaks

The law requires that employees be given breaks from their scheduled work. A 15-minute break can become 20 minutes, and 20 minutes can stretch into a half hour. If you don't spell it out in policy and enforce it, anything can happen.

Sample Policy: Breaks

Breaks of fifteen (15) minutes, morning and afternoon, are allowed for staff members working three to four consecutive hours without an intervening lunch period or other time off during an eight-hour work day. Part-time employees who work four (4) consecutive hours are allowed one 15-minute break. Breaks are not cumulative. Breaks not taken are forfeited.

Guidelines: Holidays

If the library is closed on certain holidays, the personnel policy must state what benefit employees will have as a result of the closing.

Sample Policy: Holidays

Full-time and part-time regular employees will receive their regular pay for holidays when the library is closed. When a holiday occurs Monday through Saturday, it is observed on that day. When it occurs on a Sunday, it is observed on the following Monday. Staff members whose regular day off falls on a holiday will receive compensatory time off, to be scheduled at the discretion of their department head.

Guidelines: Sick leave

The library should provide sick leave for the members of the staff. Most policies allow one working day per month for sick leave. Sick leave is sometimes allowed for illness of immediate family members, (a spouse or children).

Sample Policy: Sick leave

Full-time employees earn and accrue sick leave at the rate of one day per month, with a maximum of 100 days. Sick leave may be used for doctor or dentist visits, illness of the staff members, or, if necessary, to care for a member of the immediate family. (Immediate family is defined as spouse, children or parents.)

Hourly employees are allowed no sick leave.

Employees will not be paid for accumulated sick leave upon retirement, resignation, or dismissal.

A doctor's statement may be required in the case of any absence, or of a regular pattern of absences. (See also Absences.)

Employees who are eligible to receive Worker's Compensation because of an injury sustained on the job may elect to use their sick leave and be paid their regular salary instead of receiving worker's compensation for an injury sustained while on duty. They cannot receive both for the same time period.

All absences on sick leave for the pay period will be recorded in the Personnel Record. Sick leave absences shall be reported in increments of whole hours.

Employees who are going to be absent should notify their supervisors as early as possible, not less than fifteen (15) minutes before they are scheduled to be on duty. The supervisor will notify the business office at once. Lack of notice will forfeit sick leave privileges for that period and will be considered leave without pay that cannot be made up.

Our Library Policy: Sick leave

Guidelines: Vacations

Vacation is an earned benefit, usually granted after six months to one year of employment. Vacation length is from one week to four weeks, depending on the library, length of employment, and the professional level of the librarian and staff. If the staff member works irregular hours, the vacation should be noted in hours, not days. When a staff member is a regular employee and works a regular day, then the vacation may be stated in days.

Sample Policy: Vacations

Employees earn vacation at the rate of three weeks per year for professional staff and two weeks per year for all others. After ten years of employment, all employees earn an additional five days vacation.

Our Library Policy:

Guidelines: Other leaves of absence

Occasionally, staff members may have a need to be absent from work for personal, civic, or religious reasons (i.e., a funeral, jury duty, religious holidays, military leave, pregnancy, maternity). Whether dictated by law or for compassionate reasons, the policy should treat all employees equally. Charges of unfairness could creep in if the policy is not clearly stated and equitably administered. You can be compassionate without "giving away the farm." For example: you don't have to pay a salary or continue health insurance for six months while someone is on maternity leave. You could elect simply to hold the position open.

Sometimes staff members need to take a vacation with their spouse but have not earned the vacation necessary. Because emergencies or other situations may arise that cannot be dealt with under the regular leave of absence policy, leave of absence without pay should be allowed for up to two weeks.

Give the library director some flexibility to administer the leave policy.

Sample Policies: Other leaves of absence

Funerals: Leave with pay, up to a maximum of one week, if justified by circumstances, is allowed in case of the death of a member of the employee's immediate family. If additional time must be taken, the employee may use his or her sick leave or vacation allowance. Time off for other funerals may be granted at the discretion of the Director.

Jury Duty: Leave with pay is allowed for jury duty. However, in order to comply with state law, compensation received for jury duty must be assigned to the library if leave with pay is requested for jury duty.

Religious Holidays: An employee desiring to take time off for religious observances other than library holidays may use flex-time, or vacation time, or take the time off without pay. The absence must be scheduled with the supervisor in advance.

Military Leave: Leave of absence without pay up to one year will be granted to a member of the National Guard or Armed Forces Reserve unit ordered for military duty. Military leave of two weeks without pay will be given each year so that the employee may attend summer camp. This time will not be deducted from the employee's vacation allowance.

Pregnancy: Pregnancy will be treated as a temporary disability. Reasonable accommodation will be made for pregnant employees. Pregnant employees are expected to accept maternity leave voluntarily if a doctor determines that they are unfit to perform their tasks in the work place. The library may require and pay for an independent physician to examine any pregnant employee to determine if the woman's health will allow continued employment.

Maternity Leave: Maternity leave of up to one year without pay may be granted if requested in writing by the employee. The library may opt to rehire the employee in another position of equal status and pay when circumstances warrant it.

Leave Without Pay: One week of vacation without pay may be requested if all earned vacation has been used. This request must be submitted in writing to the library director and may be granted if the absence will not seriously affect library service.

Time Off: Part-time hourly employees may not make up time lost because they are absent, whether for illness, business, personal emergency, or any other reason.

Absences: Staff members absent for more than five (5) days in two consecutive months for any reason, except for vacation, will be subject to review and possible disciplinary action.

Our Library Policies: Other leaves of absence

Guidelines: Staff grievances

This is another area of critical importance to the board. The absence of a grievance policy could expose the board to considerable risk or even a lawsuit. Employees need an outlet for concerns that are not adequately handled by the library director.

Sample Policy: Staff grievances

Every employee shall have the privilege of submitting a grievance to the Director of the Library. If the employee is not satisfied with the settlement, he or she shall submit a written statement to the chair of the board, stating the nature of the grievance. The board chair shall arrange a personal interview or audience with the board for staff member. After consideration of the grievance, the board will render its decision in writing. Decision of the board is final.

All grievances submitted to the Board shall be considered by the Board when meeting in regular session, or in a special meeting called by the chair of the board.

Guidelines: Sexual and racial harassment

The Equal Employment Opportunity Commission (EEOC) has issued guidelines for the Commission's interpretation regarding sexual harassment as a violation of Title VII of the Civil Rights Act of 1964. Your policy should be consistent with these guidelines. Recently courts have ruled that sexual harassment has to be judged not by the standards of a "reasonable man rule," but by the standards of a "reasonable woman." This means that if a reasonable woman would consider the work place conduct of a fellow worker sexually offensive, the behavior could be ruled as sexual harassment by the courts. Any conduct that creates an intimidating, hostile, or offensive working environment should not be tolerated. Those violating this practice should be subject to disciplinary action up to and including dismissal.

In 1980 the EEOC issued guidelines that define two kinds of sexual harassment: 1) quid pro quo, i.e., the demand for sexual favors in exchange for a promotion or continued employment; and 2) a hostile environment with sexual overtones, typified by sexually overt telephone calls, electronic mail messages, and X-rated software on company computers. This type of harassment is much more difficult to detect and control.

The library's liability falls into two categories: 1) prevention and 2) resolution. The board could be liable for not having a policy in place to prevent sexual harassment, and it could be at fault for not resolving the issue. The library director could be liable for not enforcing the library's policy. The library board should create a strict policy against harassment and make sure that the library director enforces it.

Sample Policy: Sexual and racial harassment

Sexual or racial harassment is considered misconduct in the work place and could be grounds for dismissal. If it occurs, the offender will be warned. If it continues, the offender could be dismissed.

Any employee who feels that he or she has been or is being subjected to sexual or racial harassment is urged to contact the director immediately. The offended employee may contact the president of the board if the complaint is against the director. The director or the board will deal with the complaint promptly and resolve this issue.

Our Policy: Sexual and Racial Harassment

Guidelines: Substance Abuse

People who come to work while under the influence of alcohol or illegal drugs have a health problem that needs professional attention. The library has a responsibility to aid the person with an addiction in finding help.

When the addiction impairs the person's ability to perform the duties in a safe or reasonable manner, those in charge must take action to protect others and maintain the work flow. If you need to fire someone for alcoholism or drug abuse, focus on the documented performance rather than on the addiction.

All libraries receiving federal funds must have a substance abuse policy and sign assurances for a drug-free workplace.

Sample Policy: Substance Abuse Policy

1. Purpose—Employees are the Library's most valuable resource and, therefore, their health and safety is a serious concern. The library will not tolerate substance abuse or use which imperils the health and well-being of its employees or threatens its service to the public.

   The use of illegal drugs and abuse of controlled substances, on or off duty, is inconsistent with law-abiding behavior expected of all citizens. Employees who use illegal drugs or abuse controlled substances or alcohol, on or off duty, tend to be less productive, less reliable and prone to greater absenteeism resulting in the potential for increased cost, delay and risk in providing services. Ultimately, they threaten the library's ability to serve the public.

   Furthermore, employees have the right to work in a drug and alcohol free environment and to work with persons free from the effects of drug or alcohol abuse. Employees who abuse drugs or alcohol are a danger to themselves, other employees and the public. In addition, substance abuse inflicts a terrible toll on the Library's productive resources and the health and well-being of library workers and their families.

   The library is therefore committed to maintaining a safe and healthy workforce free from the influence of substance abuse and in compliance with the Federal Drug-Free Workplace Act of 1988 and to implementing rules promulgated by the United States Office of Management and Budget.
2. Policy—It shall be the policy of the library to maintain a workforce free of substance abuse.

A. Reporting to work or performing work for the library while impaired by or under the influence of illegal drugs or alcohol is prohibited.

B. The illegal use, possession, dispensation, distribution, manufacture or sale of a controlled substance by an employee at the worksite, during work hours, or while the employee is on duty, on official library business or on stand-by duty is prohibited.

C. Violation of such prohibitions by an employee is considered conduct detrimental to library service and will result in disciplinary action.

D. Employees are required by federal law to notify the employing library director or designee within five (5) days of any criminal drug statute conviction where such conviction was due to an occurrence at the worksite, during work hours, or while on duty, on official business or on stand-by duty.

   (1) An employee who is convicted of violating any criminal drug statute in such workplace situations as stated above will be subject to disciplinary action in accordance with appropriate administrative regulations.

   (2) A conviction means a finding of guilt (including a plea of nolo contendere) or the imposition of a sentence by a judge or jury, or both, in any federal state court.

E. Agencies that receive federal grants or contracts must, in turn, report any criminal drug convictions as stated above of their employees, engaged in the performance of a federal grant or contract, to federal agencies from which grants or contracts are received within (10) days after receiving notice from the employee or otherwise receiving actual notice of such conviction.

F. Current and future employees will be given a copy of the Substance Abuse Policy. Employees will be informed that they must abide by the terms of the policy as a condition of employment and of the consequences of any violation of such policy. A Substance Abuse Policy Affirmation Form will be given to employees to read and sign.

3. Assistance Program—The library encourages voluntary treatment for substance abuse. Use of the Employee Assistance Program is governed by administrative regulations. Employees wishing to avail themselves of the EAP should make an appointment with the director, through proper channels.

4. Awareness Program—The library will strive to educate employees about the dangers of substance abuse.

   The library will establish a Substance Abuse Awareness Program to assist employees to understand and avoid the perils of drug and alcohol abuse. The library will use the program in an ongoing educational effort to prevent and eliminate substance abuse that may affect the library workforce.

   The Substance Abuse Awareness Program will contain provisions to inform employees about the (1) dangers of alcohol and drug abuse; (2) library Substance Abuse Policy; (3) availability of treatment and counseling for employees who voluntarily seek such assistance; and (4) sanctions the library will impose for violations of its Substance Abuse Policy.

5. Applicability—This Substance Abuse Policy applies to all library departments. The term employees, as used in the Substance Abuse Policy, means all full-time and part-time library employees. The policy shall not be construed to prohibit or limit a drug screening program.

6. Effective Date—This Substance Abuse Policy is effective upon adoption of the personnel manual and its attachments by the governing body.

Our Policy: Substance Abuse

APPENDIX C

GREAT BEND, KANSAS, PUBLIC LIBRARY BOOK SELECTION POLICY:

Goals and Objectives

It is the goal of the Great Bend Public Library to obtain the maximum use of its collection by the greatest number of people.

The objectives of the Great Bend Public Library are: to select, organize, preserve, and to make freely available to the people of the library service area printed and other materials that will assist them to:

- Educate themselves continually
- Keep pace with progress in all fields of knowledge
- Become better members of home and community
- Develop their creative and spiritual capacities
- Appreciate works of art and literature
- Make such use of leisure time as will promote personal and social well-being
- Contribute to the growth of knowledge

Further, the Great Bend Public Library adheres to and wholly supports the Freedom to Read Statement and The Library Bill of Rights, both of which are to be considered as part of this book selection policy.

The Board of Directors has also adopted the ALA statements on 1) Reevaluating Library Collections, 2) Statement on Labeling, 3) Expurgation of Library Materials, and 4) Resolution on Challenged Materials. All four of these statements are official American Library Association interpretation of the Library Bill of Rights.

The library service area of Great Bend Public Library consists of people of all age groups, education levels, and interests. Therefore, it is the policy of the Great Bend Public Library to select books for all readers.

It is the policy of the Great Bend Public Library to cooperate with, but not perform the functions of, the school library in the community. The library's collection always seeks to complement but never to supplant the materials of the school library.

Basic Selection Criteria

The chief points considered in the selection of materials for the library are:

1. Enduring value
2. Accuracy of information
3. Authoritativeness and effectiveness of presentation
4. Literary quality
5. Social significance
6. Objectivity
7. Balance of subject areas
8. Present and future needs of the community
9. Price and availability
10. Physical format.

Contemporary and popular authors are included, as are those who have demonstrated enduring worth. Titles are selected on the basis of the content as a whole and without regard to the personal history of the author.

The library asserts its right and duty to maintain on its shelves a representative selection of books on all subjects of interest to its readers not prohibited specifically by law, including books on all sides of controversial issues. The library will not emphasize one subject at the expense of another, or one side of a subject without regard to the other side. It will attempt to provide the important books on all sides and subjects within the limitations of space and budget.

The library will not identify, through the use of labels or other devices, particular philosophies or moral situations expressed in a book.

To preserve valuable human expression and documents, it is necessary to judge a book on more than its literary merits and scholarship. Penetrating, impartial, and critical judgment must include:

1. The degree of accomplishment of purpose
2. The authority and competence of the author
3. Comprehensiveness
4. Sincerity and fundamental objectivity
5. Readability
6. Potential usefulness
7. Relation to the existing collection
8. Importance as a record of the times
9. Importance in comparison with other books on the subject

10. New and worthwhile information to the library
11. Availability of contents, indexes, and bibliographic material.

Reprints of older or out-of-print works are purchased subject to the criteria of good book selection.

Memorial and/or commemorative editions are purchased only when they will add notably to the stature of the library collection or when they are of local interest.

As the amount of money to be spent for books is not large, no special collections are consciously developed.

Books of local and state history are acquired, but no attempt is made to have a historically comprehensive Kansas collection.

Leisure reading may be either fact or fiction.

These are criteria for selecting books for leisure:

1. Invigorating quality
2. Artistic expression
3. Originality and imagination
4. Honesty of presentation
5. Physical construction
6. Interesting presentation/style
7. Good characterization
8. Timeliness.

Bestsellers are considered on individual merits.

Popular authors are considered on the merits of the individual work.

Children's Books

The basic policy of book selection for children is to choose the best new books and replace and duplicate only those older titles that are considered important. The selection includes books for recreational reading, inspirational books of lasting value, and books of information covering a wide range of knowledge that will satisfy the child's natural curiosity and widen his or her interests. Each book is judged on its own merits; and is considered also in relation to the collection as a whole and in relation to the children for whom it is intended. Special attention must be paid to the illustrations and the physical qualities (binding, paper, etc.). Size of print and vocabulary development are especially important to consider in children's books for the very young.

In the selection of children's books it must be remembered that parents may want to send their children to the library to select books on their own, and indeed part of the learning and growing-up process for children is to be able to select books for themselves. Libraries should be sensitive to parents needs concerning adequate information about sex education. The library should not hesitate to purchase materials for children to be used by adults in the process of teaching sex education in the home.

Gifts

The library has been favored by public-spirited citizens as a beneficiary of gifts. Since such additions to our revenues assist us in carrying out our purposes, they are always encouraged and welcomed.

1. **Gifts of money:** Tax revenues are the normal source of income for all public libraries. Gifts and endowments are encouraged to enrich and expand library programs. Such gifts are tax deductible.
2. **Gifts of books or other materials:** Materials selected for the library's collection must meet high selection criteria on the basis of literary quality and usefulness. Gift materials are screened by the same standards as are all other materials; therefore, the library's acceptance of a gift is not a guarantee that such gift will be processed into the regular collections and made available to the public. Such gifts as are found acceptable are cataloged and placed in their regular places on the shelves where they are most useful, rather than in a special gift collection. Although special book plates are inserted to identify gifts and memorials when requested, gifts are considered part of the regular collection.

By accepting and using such gifts, the library assumes no special obligations to the donors. Gifts which do not meet the library's selection criteria are disposed of in whatever ways the library sees fit.

The library does not accept for permanent deposit materials which are not given as outright gifts.

The final responsibility for the selection of materials at Great Bend Public Library rests with the library director, assisted by staff members, operating within the framework of policies adopted by the library board. Suggestions from readers and board members are always welcomed and will be given serious consideration.

Whenever possible, those people in the community who have special education or talents in a specific area would be used as subject consultants in the choice of books.

Ideally, every book added to the library would be read before purchase by a librarian with trained judgment, knowledge of the library's present resources, and acquaintance with the requirements of local readers. Where circumstances make such reading impossible or unnecessary, the staff makes skilled use of selection aids such as basic general lists, current general lists, special bibliographies for reference books and particular subject materials, and book reviewing journals. While book reviews are a major source of information about new books, they are not followed blindly. No one publication is relied upon exclusively.

Withdrawals

In order to maintain a vital, interesting, and usable collection, the Great Bend Public Library continually removes from its collection items which through usage or the passage of time are no longer suitable for use or are no longer necessary. The following criteria will be used when considering material for withdrawal:

1. *Volumes of no use to the library:* If a title has gone three to five years without circulating, has not to the librarian's knowledge been used in the library for reference purposes, and is not a standard title, it would probably warrant discarding. Even classics, if unused because of unattractive appearance, should be replaced with better editions.
2. *Books of poor content:* This applies to such material as: outdated information (applies especially in the sciences, medicine, geography, technology, and travel); trivial subject matter or a trivial approach to it; mediocrity of writing; false information; unused volumes of sets; repetitious series, particularly in the children's field; superseded editions. Unneeded duplicate titles of fiction and nonfiction as well as superfluous books in subject fields in which the community has little interest will also be removed.
3. *Books of very poor appearance:* This includes badly bound and printed editions (small print, shoddy binding, dull print, cramped margins, poor illustrations, pulpy paper through which the print shows); worn-out books (yellowed, and brittle paper, mutilated or missing pages, frayed bindings, broken backs, dingy or dirty covers);. and sets whose antiquated appearance discourages use.

It shall be the responsibility of the librarian employed by the board of directors to use his or her own knowledge of books and the advisory assistance available to him or her, when necessary or possible, to make the decision to remove materials from the shelves and dispose of them in a suitable manner.

(Source: Great Bend Kansas Public Library Book Selection Policy).

Note: Larger libraries may need a more elaborate book selection policy. Smaller libraries may not need such an extensive policy. Generally, smaller libraries could not afford to acquire books "on all subjects from all points of view." They may wish to develop their collection based "on current topics with representative points of view."

APPENDIX D

INFORMATION FOR NEW EMPLOYEES

Welcome to the library staff. We want to make your experience here a positive one. You have been given a copy of the personnel policy. Please take the time to read it soon. If you have questions, please ask your supervisor. Here are some items that may not be in the personnel policy, but are nevertheless important. They are meant to help you "learn the ropes" of working in the library.

Check In and Out: Your name is on our in-out board. You are required to move your button "in" when you report for work or when you return from being out of the building. Move your button "out" when you leave the building for the day. Put your button on the time that you will be returning any time that you leave the building.

Work Schedule: The office needs your weekly work schedule by Friday of each week. If you plan to be away from work on Friday, fill out your schedule in advance for the coming weeks. Once your schedule is set, you are expected to report to work as scheduled.

Absences: If you are not coming in as scheduled, you must call to notify the office before you are scheduled to be in. You must call in each day you are absent.

Sick Leave/Vacation Forms: You need to fill out an absence report form when you return to work from sick leave or other absences. You are eligible for vacation after six months of employment. Fill out the vacation request form before your vacation is scheduled. Both of these forms will be used to account for your time off.

Severe Weather Closing: The library will be closed if U.S.D. 428 schools are closed because of bad weather. If the schools close early on a snow day, you may use flex-time to transport your children home if necessary. If you choose not to come to work because of the weather and the library is open, you may use flex-time or a vacation day for the day you missed. If the library is closed due to bad weather, you could be called to work if the weather improves.

Staff Meetings: These are usually scheduled at the convenience of those involved. If a staff meeting is scheduled for a day you are not at work, you are not required to attend. If you do attend on your day off, you may count the time in attendance as flex-time.

Paydays-Paycheck: Payday is the 30th of the month or the Friday before if the 30th falls on a weekend. You must come to the office in person to get your check. If you are not at work on payday, we will hold your check or deposit it in a local bank for you. With your signed authorization, we will give your check to a person you designate. Do not ask for your check early.

Accidents on the Job: Any accidents should be reported to the office immediately, with a follow-up report in writing as soon as possible after the occurrence.

Parking: Parking is permitted anywhere around the library except near the trash collection bin or the book drop. You may be asked to move your car if it is parked in one of the parallel spaces behind the southwest corner of the library. The Rotating Book Truck is usually parked there when it is not out.

Smoking: Smoking is restricted to the smoking lounge. A "smoke break" away from your desk counts as your break for the morning or afternoon.

Visits: Friends and family members should not interfere with your work. When using the library, they should stay in the public area. Your children may not come to work with you because you don't have a sitter for them. Family visits to your work area should be limited in frequency and in duration.

Personal Use of the Telephone: You should make local calls only and limit them in number and duration. Please encourage your family members to limit their calls you at work. If you must make a long distance calls from work, charge it to your home telephone or calling card.

Photocopies: Staff members pay 5 cents per copy for copies they make for personal use.

Staff Circulation Policy: Staff members have indefinite loan privileges. That means you don't have to bring your books back on time or pay fines. You will be asked to return a book on the normal due date if it has a request on it. Please have the circulation staff check out your books; do not do it yourself.

Professional Memberships: The library will pay for your membership in appropriate professional library associations. This benefit is based on your potential for attendance at annual meetings. Check with the office if you have questions.

Staff Association Membership: This membership is open to all employees of the library except library administration. Dues are $1 per year. Meetings are held monthly in the lounge.

Use of Equipment in Your Area: You may use the typewriter or other equipment in your work area for personal use, provided you use it in the library and on your own time.

Banking: The library does not cash checks. If you need a large bill changed, there are two banks within one block of the library.

Health Products: The library will furnish facial tissues for your work area.

The Staff Lounge: Two refrigerators and a microwave oven are provided by the Staff Association. A vending machine contains soda pop. Clean up after yourself. Dirty cups and dishes are your responsibility, not the responsibility of the housekeeper.

APPENDIX E

DEFINITION OF ADMINISTRATIVE ROLES BY POSITION

Clearly defined roles lead to better communication and delegation of authority. This document is designed to help staff members understand their roles and the authority delegated to them regarding the administration of the library. It is designed for board members and staff at all levels.

Inherent with every responsibility is the authority to carry out the tasks involved. Accountability is essential to delegation. The Board is accountable to the people; the director is accountable to the Board; the assistant director is accountable to the director and so on. Each of the headings listed represents an area of responsibility that must be defined to make sure the organization runs smoothly.

Budget Preparation

Each year a budget is prepared by the director in coordination with the Board. The staff makes recommendations early in the process. A preliminary budget is prepared in the spring and tentatively approved by the Board in September. A final budget is approved in January after expenditures from the previous year have been processed. The Board's budget committee reviews all proposed line items and programs.

Director: Prepares the tentative budget at all phases. Reviews it with assistant director before it goes to the board. Works with Budget Committee as resource person. Explains the budget at the board meeting. Delegates funds to departments for expenditures after the final budget has been approved.

Assistant Director: Recommends changes with target amounts to the director during the preparation of the budget before it goes to the board. Reviews budget with the director before final approval.

Administrative Assistant: Recommends changes with target amounts to the director for budget categories which have been specifically delegated to the Business Office.

Department Heads: Recommend changes with target amounts to assistant director for specifically delegated categories for the department by November 1 of each year.

Support Staff: Recommend changes in the budget for the department to the department head.

Budget Management

After the budget has been approved by the Board, funds are delegated to department heads to carrying out the functions of their departments. Each staff member who has been delegated the responsibility for the expenditure of funds will fill out purchase orders according to Purchase Order Guidelines.

A budget expresses projected revenues and projected expenses. End-of-the-year flexibility is important in the event of unforeseen expenditures or revenue shortfalls. While allowances are made for seasonal or annual lump sum expenditures it is generally advisable to stay within the suggested percentages on a month-by-month basis; (e.g., 50 percent by June 30, 75 percent by September 30). Each staff member who has the authority of delegated funds is responsible for staying within the allocated budget, including encumbrances.

Director: Responsible to the board for all expenditures. Reviews and signs purchase orders before purchases are made. Reviews and authorizes payment after purchases are received and assigns expenditure code if one has not been assigned by the person generating the purchase order. May generate original purchase orders for central administration. Approves all capital outlay expenditures.

Assistant Director: Generates purchase orders for delegated funds according to purchase order guidelines. May assist or instruct other staff members in creating a purchase order. Maintains records of expenditures for delegated funds including encumbrances.

Administrative Assistant: Generates purchase orders for delegated funds according to purchase order guidelines. Sorts incoming invoices and routes them to departments for verification of goods or services received or the generation of a purchase order not previously created. May assist or instruct staff members in the preparation of purchase orders. Works with accounts assistant in the preparation of purchase orders that cannot be allocated to a specific department.

Department Heads: Generate purchase orders for delegated funds according to purchase order guidelines. Verify receipt of goods or services in invoices. Maintain personal records of expenditures for delegated funds, including encumbrances.

Accounts Assistant: Generate purchase orders according to purchase order guidelines for expenditures that cannot be routed to a specific department. Maintains a file of purchase orders and follows other instructions as outlined in the purchase order guidelines.

Support Staff: Generates purchase orders according to purchase order guidelines for the department when asked to do so by the department head.

Board Meetings

The board is legally responsible for the operation of the library. Board meetings are held once a month to carry out the business of the library. The agenda usually includes approval of minutes, expenditures, and reports from the director and various board committees. The board gives careful attention to the budget and the expenditure of funds. The board makes decisions about policy, the budget, the salary schedule, major purchases, and program changes. The board meeting is a time for sharing information so that board members can make informed decisions.

The board has delegated the responsibility for day-to-day operation to the director. The board meeting is a time for the director to report and receive feedback from the board about the operation of the library. Decisions made at board meetings will be reported to the staff by the director or through the minutes of the meeting.

Director: Attends all board meetings, produces written report and comments on it at the board meeting. Is responsible for the financial statement and other special reports. Recommends policy changes, budget allocations, major purchases, and new programs. May answer questions and participate in the general discussion at board meetings when information he or she has will contribute to the understanding of individual board members.

Assistant Director: Prepares a written report to be mailed with the packet prior to the board meeting. Participates in board meetings if he or she has specific information for the board.

Administrative Assistant: Attends all board meetings and acts as the recording secretary. Writes the minutes of the previous meeting for approval by the board. Prepares reports for the director and other staff members as submitted. Prepares other documents for board meetings as needed. Calls board members to remind them of board meetings and ascertains which members will attend the meeting.

Department Heads: Prepare brief reports for board by the Tuesday of the week before the board meeting. Reports includes statistical data and comparisons with last year as well as reports of recent and ongoing activities.

Support Staff: Assist in the preparation of departmental reports.

Policy

The establishment of policy is a board function. Policies are determined as a blueprint or guide for stable operation of the system. Broad areas of policy include: services, personnel, the budget, public relations, hours, loan periods, insurance, salary schedules, book selection and use of facilities. The list can be very long. Policies are reviewed periodically to make sure they accomplish their intent. Generally, staff has input on policy in the beginning of the process. Once policy has been established, it should be observed until it is changed.

Director: Is responsible for recommending policy to the board and carrying out policy once established. May produce administrative guidelines for policy implementation. Responsible for the interpretation of policy to staff.

Assistant Director: Recommends policy changes to the director.

Administrative Assistant: Recommends policy changes to the director.

Department Heads: Recommend policy changes to the assistant director.

Support Staff: Recommend policy changes to department head.

Staff Selection

Staff selection is important to the success of the organization. Hiring and firing is a task specifically delegated by the board to the director. We like to participate in the decision to hire or not to hire the people in our department. Every person who is hired by the Library is offered a salary that must be set by the director.

The recruiting process is as follows: (1) The job is advertised in the newspaper, through the job service, or in a professional journal. (2) A period of time is allowed for written applications. (3) All applications are reviewed, and qualified applicants that best match the job requirements are invited to the library for an interview. They are interviewed by two people who make the final selection. A job is offered to the person selected. If he or she accepts, letters are sent to the unsuccessful applicants after the new person starts work.

The first interviewer usually explains the job to the interviewee, answers questions and makes general observations about the person. The interviewee is then brought to the office of the second interviewer, who asks questions about such things as past employment, and the interviewee's ideas about the job in question, and determines the expected salary, answers questions, and explains the fringe benefits. The first interviewer is usually a department head or assistant director. The second interviewer is usually the assistant director or the director.

Director: Writes the job advertisement. Reviews all applications with the assistant director and appropriate department head, if applicable. Assists in the decision of those to be interviewed. Is the last interviewer for assistant director, department heads and business office staff. Establishes salaries for all employees.

Assistant Director: Reviews all applications with the director and department head, when applicable. Participates in the screening of applications and is the first interviewer for business office staff. Trains new employees after they are hired and forwards payroll information to bookkeeper.

Department Heads: Participate in the screening of applications for their department. Are first interviewers for support staff within the department. Make decision for employment with assistant director.

Support Staff: Make informal observations about applicants and share them with the department head. May be invited to lunch with applicant at the time of the interview, if applicable.

Staff Supervision

Staff supervision means coordinating the work of others. To the fullest extent possible, staff supervision means helping staff members learn their roles and then letting them do their job. In this sense every staff member becomes a supervisor, because we all set goals and objectives for ourselves and work to accomplish them.

Staff supervision is working with individuals to achieve the goals of the organization. This coordinating effort causes the supervisor to view the broad goals of the library while focusing on the specific objectives and tasks of the department. The organizational goal of the library is to give the people what they want when they come to the library. Our specific objectives should always support that goal.

Director: Responsible to the board for over all supervision of the staff. Works with the board to set organizational goals. Works together with assistant director, when necessary to solve problems or make decisions. Reviews six-month and 12-month performance reports with staff members. Informally visits with staff members about activities in their departments. Accessible to staff. Handles staff grievances.

Assistant Director: Works with department heads to set long-range goals and short-term objectives. Formally monitors the work and progress of each department and makes necessary changes. Recommends changes in responsibilities and task assignments. Completes six-month and 12-month performance reviews on newly appointed department heads. Informs the director of ongoing staff activities. Is the first contact for department heads in problem solving that cannot be resolved within the department.

Administrative Assistant: Maintains good communications between the business office and all other departments. Supervises business office staff. Maintains personnel files and records. Prepares timely reports for staff on the use of sick leave, vacation, and the like. Initiates six-month and 12-month reviews for all newly appointed staff and routes them to the appropriate supervisor.

Department Heads: Supervise the work of departmental staff members. Work with other department heads to accomplish goals of mutual interest. Responsible for establishing goals and objectives of the department in coordination with the assistant director. Complete six-month and 12-month performance reviews for newly appointed departmental staff. Forward reviews to the director with a copy to the assistant director. Review objectives regularly with assistant director.

Support Staff: Responsible to the department head to accomplish the objectives of the department. Recommends changes in task performance to department head.

Staff Development

Staff development will enhance an individual's skills, abilities, or performance. System personnel must regularly reassess their knowledge, skills, and attitudes if they are to remain competent in their positions. This two-way responsibility requires the organization to support educational opportunities and requires the employee to expend time and energy to gain the additional knowledge and training.

For some employees staff development may be a class at the local community college; for others it will be attendance at a state or national conference. It could be a special workshop on staff supervision or computers or consulting. The board has established policy governing staff development. It will be followed to determine the kinds and extent of activities that will be supported and funded.

Director: Recommends adequate funding in the budget for staff development. Delegates to assistant director the responsibility of determining which department heads and support staff go to which activities. The director usually attends state, regional and national conferences annually, and funds permitting, attends one or two workshops or other staff development activities each year. Meets with assistant director after final budget is set to determine potential costs, set priorities, and plan for continuing education.

Assistant Director: Responsible for overall staff training and development. Encourages specific staff development activities for department heads and support staff. Confers with the director for assistance in decision making. May be a workshop leader for in-house continuing education activities. According to availability of funds may, attend state, regional, or national conferences. May attend workshops of special interest appropriate to responsibilities.

Administrative Assistant: Keeps abreast of knowledge in the area of office management and technology. May attend state library conferences and specialized workshops. Maintains files of staff continuing education activities.

Department Heads: Keep abreast of knowledge in the discipline of the department. Actively pursue opportunities for training and development. May attend state library conferences and local or state workshops. Encouraged to attend system workshops, and classes at the community college or other institutions of higher education whenever appropriate classes are offered.

Support Staff: Keep abreast of knowledge in the disciplines of the department. May occasionally attend state library conferences. Encouraged to attend system workshops and appropriate classes at the community college or other institution of higher education.

Staff Meetings

Staff meetings are efficient means of communicating events in the organization. Everyone should make an effort to attend staff meetings for which their attendance has been called. Types of staff meetings are: 1) general staff meetings—everyone in the building is involved; 2) department head meetings—just the department heads; 3) support staff meetings—just support staff and one administrator; 4) administrative staff meetings—just the director, the assistant director, and the administrative assistant. Other combinations of staff members may be called together to discuss a particular problem or plan for a given project.

Some staff meetings are held on a regular basis. Others are called as the need arises. Although generally they are called by the administrative staff, others may request a special staff meeting and allow all participants time enough to schedule for it. The person calling a meeting is responsible for informing the participants that the meeting is about to start. Anyone may be asked to chair a staff meeting.

Director: Calls and conducts general staff meetings for everyone in the building. Calls and conducts administrative staff meetings. Is informed about *all* other staff meetings; may attend at his or her discretion.

Assistant Director: Schedules and attends department head meetings. Calls and conducts meetings with support staff. Checks the director's schedule before scheduling staff meeting. Responsible for the agenda. Informs all participants when a meeting is about to begin. Ends all staff meetings before participants are scheduled to leave work either for lunch or the end of the day.

Administrative Assistant: Attends and takes minutes of administrative meetings. Attends general staff meetings. May choose to attend other staff meetings.

Department Heads: Attend general staff meetings, department head meetings, and general meetings. May be asked to conduct a department head meeting occasionally.

Support Staff: Attend general and support staff meetings.

Community Relations

One of the main objectives of the library is to make its patrons aware of its services. This function can be performed at various levels by all staff members and trustees. The success of the organization will depend on how well this is done. All staff members are expected to be pleasant and professional in their approach to people, whether in person or on the telephone.

If a person is hostile or is seeking an "official" interpretation of policy, he or she should be referred to the director or the assistant director.

Director: Stays in touch with board members and librarians in the area. Seeks opportunities to conduct programs to promote the services of the library. Plans and conducts training sessions for trustees. Is the *official* link between the board and the staff. Officially interprets system policy for trustees, other librarians and patrons. Maintains personal visibility in the community and the System. Deals with hostile patrons or questioners.

Assistant Director: Stays in touch with librarians in the area. Seeks opportunities to conduct programs to promote the services of the library. Maintains personal visibility in the area. Deals with hostile patrons or questions, as needed.

Administrative Assistant: Stays informed about events and developments in the library that may have an impact upon services.

May provide factual policy information. Refers policy interpretation questions or hostile patrons to the director or assistant director.

Department Heads: Stay informed about events and developments in the library that may have an impact upon services. Should be willing to present programs or workshops that promote services of the department. May provide factual policy information. Refer policy interpretation questions or hostile patrons to the director or assistant director.

Support Staff: Promote a positive image for the library. May be asked to participate in a workshop or on a program relating to department. Refer policy interpretation questions or hostile patrons to the director, or assistant director.

Collection Development

While staff has been described as the heart and soul of a library operation, books and materials are the blood that flows through the veins. Without staff, patrons may not get what they want. Without adequate materials they surely will not get what they want. Every collection is unique and should reflect the needs of the users. Those delegated to select books and materials for a library collection have important responsibilities. The people who decide which materials to buy consider several factors: 1) the current collection; 2) the materials selection policy as adopted by the Board; 3) the audience that will use the materials; and 4) the materials that are available in print. Staff members who make selections decisions should be the same people who work with patrons on a regular basis.

Unfortunately, we cannot inspect every book, film, and other material purchase. Therefore, it is important that selectors read review journals to stay abreast of new materials. This is a regular part of the job for those staff members who have the responsibility for selecting materials.

Director: Recommends materials selections policy to the Board. Delegates funds to appropriate staff members for the purchase of materials. May recommend books for purchase to appropriate staff members. Establishes guidelines for the purchase of second, third or fourth copies of popular titles. May select materials for the professional collection.

Assistant Director: May recommend materials selection policies to the director. Is familiar with current materials and selection policy and selects materials accordingly. Selects materials for purchase for the professional collection staying within the budget delegated for the purpose. Monitors book selections made by other staff members.

Administrative Assistant: May select professional development materials relating to the Business Office. May recommend materials selection policies to the director.

Department Heads: Maintain knowledge of materials selection policy and the needs of the users. Maintain familiarity with collection. Keep abreast of upcoming materials. Select and purchase materials from delegated funds.

Support Staff: Maintain knowledge of current materials selection policy. Make selection suggestions to department head. May be asked to type orders.

Building Maintenance

All staff members are primarily concerned about the following: 1) appearance; 2) heating and cooling; 3) safety; 4) security. If any one of these factors is compromised, we need to do something about it. The building engineer is responsible to the director for all of these factors. Any condition that needs attention should be mentioned to the director or the building engineer.

The urgency of a safety problem or a security situation may require a staff member to take action immediately, in which case he or she has full authority to act in the best interest of the library to insure the safety of the staff and patrons or the security of the building.

Director: Responsible to the board for the appearance, safety and security of the library building. Works with the building engineer to carry out this stewardship. Authorizes major expenditures to maintain the appearance, heating and cooling, safety, and security of the building. Supervises building engineer.

Administrative Assistant: Authorizes urgent or emergency repairs in the absence of the director.

Building Engineer: Responsible to the director for the appearance, comfort, safety and security of the building and grounds. Calls the environmental controls technician, the plumber and the electrician to maintain proper temperature, plumbing, and electrical functions. Reports such activities and other conditions to the director and the Business Office. Supervises the housekeeper.

Housekeeper: Maintains the cleanliness of the building. Responsible to the building engineer.

All Other Staff Members: Report unfavorable conditions to the building engineer or the director. If an emergency occurs and the director, the building engineer, and the administrative assistant are absent, staff members may act to remedy an urgent condition and report it to the administration. Each staff member is responsible for the appearance of his or her individual work area. The last person to leave the building should turn off the lights and make sure the building is locked.

Professional Activities and Library Awareness

All staff members are expected to be aware of developments in librarianship and other disciplines appropriate to their department. This can be done by reading journals and attending meetings and conferences. Since it may not be possible to perform all of these activities on library time, we could spend some time at home reading *American Libraries, Library Journal, Wilson Library Bulletin,* or other professional journals. If attending a conference at library expense, staff members are expected to use personal time if the event occurs on Saturday or Sunday.

Professional activities such as serving on a committee or running for office are important to professional growth. Staff members are encouraged to do so whenever asked. However, it should be remembered that professional activities take away from our work time and can be a financial liability to the organization. All staff members should discuss these implications with the director before agreeing to serve on any committee or run for office in a professional organization.

APPENDIX F

CASE STUDY

You are the president of your library board. The mayor, Mary Farley, has just called you on the telephone. Her first words were, "You'd better do something about that librarian of yours before I strangle her." Then for the next 30 minutes you listen to the mayor's list of complaints.

As soon as you hang up, the librarian, Jane Eyre, calls you. She has just had an "ugly scene" with the mayor. This is not the first time. Your job is to sort things out and resolve the conflict.

The Mayor's Story

"I went to the library this afternoon to return a book I had just finished. I no sooner got in the door than Jane began yelling at me about the book. She said that she had a waiting list on the book and it was getting longer every day. She said the fine would be $1. That's when I got upset. I've been mayor of this town for 10 years, and I have never paid a library fine. This new librarian is a trouble maker. She is just making changes too fast. She doesn't know how we do things around here.

"Well, when I told her I never paid library fines, she got huffy and told me that everyone had to pay fines on overdue books—no exceptions. Then I said, "What about the people who put their overdue books in the book drop?" Then she really got mad. She let out a stream of complaints against me and the city council that she must have been saving for months. She said that I hated the library and that we stifled any efforts to increase the library's budget.

"And you remember this: Last month at the council meeting when we were working on the budget, she packed the gallery with library supporters to lobby in favor of the budget. No one has ever done that before. She wouldn't even let us work on the budget in peace. Can you imagine the confusion if every city department did that?

"Well, anyway, if you don't do something about your librarian, I'll fire her myself, and I told her that."

The Librarian's Story

"The Mayor came into the library this afternoon and created a terrible scene. She threatened to fire me.

"I guess it started with her overdue book. She had the latest Danielle Steel novel. It was four weeks overdue. I know she has already read it. She was just passing it around among her special friends, and there's a waiting list of 20 people who want to read it. We sent her two notices, and my assistant called her once. She said that she would return the book when she finished it.

"Well, today when she returned it, she got really mad when I tried to charge her a dollar for the fine. She said that she had been mayor for 10 years and she has never paid a library fine. Who does she think she is anyway?

"I guess I said some dumb things about her and the city council. Who could help it after the way we were treated at the city council meeting last month? Did you know that we are going to lose $10,000 in our budget next year? And it is all because of the mayor and that new city administrator. He says that the city can't give the library any more than what the mill levy yields. For the past two years the council voted to supplement the library's mill levy with money from the general fund. Now we will probably lose state aid.

"Just before she left, she threatened to fire me if I didn't stop meddling in city business and making it hard for the council to do its job."

Other Facts

Jane Eyre has been librarian for a year and a half. She has done a good job. Since she took over, circulation has increased 25 percent. Her reports to the board are always well prepared.

Bill Sykes has been the city administrator for six months. He has been given the responsibility of keeping the city's mill levy at last year's level, even though the assessed valuation is down eight percent. He is taking his job seriously.

Bill is the first person to occupy the position of city administrator. Until he came to the job, the mayor and the city clerk handled many of the responsibilities he now assumes.

Assignment

You are a close personal friend of the mayor, Mary Farley. She is a person who believes she is always right; the librarian is almost as inflexible. You fear that a serious rift between the city and the library is developing. Your job is to come to the workshop prepared to discuss the situation and make recommendations for resolving the conflict .

Note: The case study is designed to stimulate discussion, and it is the creation of the author's imagination, based on incidents he has witnessed. The names are made up, too.

BIBLIOGRAPHY

Ahearn, Ellen T. "Feedback Interviews," *Supervisor's Bulletin*, August 30, 1987.

Alvarez, Robert S. *Library Log: The Diary of a Public Library Director*, Foster City, CA: Administrator's Digest Pr., 1991.

American Library Association, 1979. Small Libraries Publication No. 1.

Ashfield, Jean A. *Friends of the Library Handbook*. Somersworth, NH: Friends of New Hampshire Libraries, 1980.

Bader, Barbara C. & Steven Carr. *Enhancing Board Effectiveness: Working with Boards, Councils and Committees*, Bozeman, MT: Community Systems, 1989.

Berry, John, "The Crucial Relationship," *Library Journal*, April 4, 1988, p. 4.

Bird, Roy, *The Handy Book for Kansas Public Librarians & Trustees*, Topeka , KS: Kansas State Library, 1991.

Board Member Trustee Handbook, San Francisco: Public Management Institute, 1980.

Bolt, Nancy. *Evaluating the Library Director*. Chicago: American Library Trustee Assn., American Library Assn., 1983. ALTA Publication, No. 6.

Bolton, Robert, *People Skills: How to Assert Yourself, Listen to Others and Resolve Conflicts*, Englewood Cliffs, NJ: Prentice-Hall, 1979.

Covey, Stephen R. *How to Succeed with People*, Salt Lake City, UT: Deseret Book, 1972.

————. *Seven Basic Habits of Highly Effective People*, Provo, UT: Stephen R. Covey and Assoc., 1989. (Audiocassette Seminar)

————. *The 7 Habits of Highly Effective People*, New York, Simmon & Schuster, 1989.

————. *Principle-Centered Leadership*, New York, Summit Bks., 1991.

Curzon, Susan C. *Managing Change: A How-To-Do-It Manual for Planning, Implementing and Evaluating Change in Libraries*. New York, Neal-Schuman Publishers, 1989.

Dolnick, Sandy, ed. *Friends of Libraries Sourcebook*. Chicago: American Library Assn., 1988.

Edie, John A. *First Steps in Starting a Foundation.* Washington, DC.: Council on Foundations, 1987.

Executive Office of the President, Office of Management and Budget. *1989 Catalog of Federal Domestic Assistance.* Washington, DC.: U.S. General Services Admin., 1989.

Foundation Center, *Grants for Libraries and Information Services.* New York: The Foundation Center, 1989.

Gervasi, Anne & Betty Kay Seibt. *Handbook for Small, Rural, and Emerging Public Libraries.* Phoenix, Oryx Pr., 1988.

Hackler, Eugene T. *Legal and Practical Aspects of Boardsmanship,* Published privately (P.O. Box 1, Olathe, KS 66061)

Hall, Mary. *Getting Funded: A Complete Guide to Proposal Writing.* 3rd ed. Portland, ME: Continuing Education Publications, Portland State Univ., 1988.

Ihrig, Alice B. *Decision Making for Public Libraries,* Hamden, CT, Shoe String Pr., 1989.

Indiana State Library. *Multiple Choice.* 16mm film, 25 min. 1972. (o.p.). May be available on interlibrary loan.

Interviewing Made Easy: The Right Way to Ask Hiring Questions. Maywood, NJ: No Date.

Kadanoff, Diane Gordon. "Small Libraries—No Small Job! " *Library Journal,* March 1, 1986, p. 72-73.

Lynch, Timothy P. "A Preliminary Survey of Library Board Trustees from Four Libraries in Pennsylvania," *Rural Libraries,* (Vol. VII, no. 11) 1987, p. 61-97.

McClure, Charles R., Amy Owen, Douglas Zweizig, et. al. *Planning and Role Setting for Public Libraries.* Chicago, American Library Assn., 1987.

Meyer, Richard W. "How to Read an Applicant Resume," *Administrative Management,* February 1987. No page.

Naisbitt, John. *Megatrends.* New York: Warner Bks., 1984.

O'Connell, Brian. *The Board Member's Book.* New York: The Foundation Center, 1985.

Performance Appraisals: The Latest Legal Nightmare, Alexander Hamilton Institute, Maywood, NJ, 1989.

Public Library Policy Resource Manual, Lansing, MI: Michigan Library Assn., No date.

Richards, Audrey, series ed. *Board Member Trustee Handbook*. San Francisco: Public Management Institute, 1980.

Robert, Henry M. *Robert's Rules of Order, Newly revised*, (9th Ed.) Scott, Foresman, 1990.

Stanton, Erwin S. *Successful Personnel Recruiting and Selection: With EEO/ Affirmative Action Guidelines*, New York, AMACOM, 1977.

Swan, James. "Bend But Don't Break, " *Newsletter on Intellectual Freedom*, November 1981, No. 6, 160f.

————. "Fund-raising for the Small Public Library," *Wilson Library Bulletin*, April 1989, p. 46-48,

————. *Fundraising for the Small Public Library: A How-To-Do-It Manual for the Librarian*, New York, Neal-Schuman Publishers, 1990.

————. "Grass Roots Fundraising," *The Bottom Line: A Financial Magazine for Librarians,* Vol. III No. 3, 1989, p. 31-32.

————. "Inside the System: A Primer for Trustees,: *Wilson Library Bulletin*, February 1986, p. 27-30.

————. "New Visibility for the Small PL," *Wilson Library Bulletin*, January 1977, p. 424-27.

————. "Placemats in Restaurants," in *68 Great Ideas: The Library Awareness Handbook,* Chicago: American Library Assn., 1982.

————. *Trustee Handbook: A Practical Guide for the Library Trustee,* Central Kansas Library System. Great Bend, KS, 1987. (Privately published)

————. *Trustee Orientation Workshop Workbook,* Central Kansas Library System. Great Bend, KS, 1989. (Privately published)

Swan, Walter, *How to Be a Better Me: A Philosophical Approach to Living a Successful Life,* Bisbee, AZ: Swan Enterprises, 1991.

Van House, Nancy A., Mary Jo Lynch, Charles R. McClure, et al. *Output*

Measures for Public Libraries. 2nd ed. Chicago: American Library Assn., 1987.

Wilson, Marlene. *The Effective Management of Volunteer Programs.* Boulder, CO: Volunteer Management Assoc., 1976.

Yarbrough, Elaine, *Identifying Interests in Conflict* (Workshop handout) Boulder, CO: Yarbrough and Assoc., 1988.

Young, Virginia. *The Library Trustee: A Practical Guidebook* (3d ed.) New York: Bowker, 1978.

———. *The Library Trustee: A Practical Guidebook* (4th ed.) Chicago: American Library Assn., 1988.

INDEX

James Swan is Director of the Central Kansas Library System, Great Bend, Kansas. He is also the author of *Fundraising for the Small Public Library, A How-To-Do-It Manual for Librarians.*

Book design: Gloria Brown
Cover design: Gregory Apicella
Typography: C. Roberts